Victim, Survivor, or Navigator?

Choosing a Response to
Workplace Change

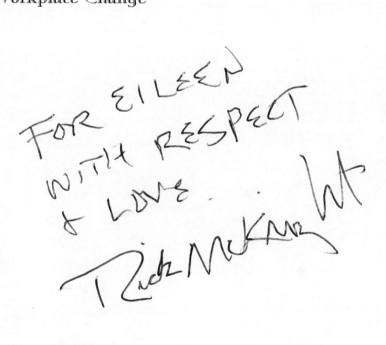

FOR EILEEN
WITH RESPECT
& LOVE...

Rick McKnight

Victim, Survivor, or Navigator?

Choosing a Response to Workplace Change

Richard McKnight, Ph.D.

TrueNorth Press
Philadelphia, PA

Published by TrueNorth Press, Philadelphia, PA
Copyright © 2010, Richard McKnight, Ph.D.

McKnight, Richard, 1947–
Victim, survivor, or navigator / Richard McKnight.
Philadelphia : True North Press, 2010.
 p. : ill. ; cm.
Summary: A guide for employees in making the best of workplace change.
Includes index.
ISBN 978-0-9824683-0-2
LIbrary of Congress control number 2009931991
1. Career changes. 2. Vocational guidance. I. Title.

Table of Contents

What Others Have Said about this Book

Richard McKnight brings a deep understanding of how individuals respond to change and connects it to the context of organizational life. In this concise and well-written book, he lays out a framework that will be useful to anyone who is struggling with the stress of organizational uncertainty.

—*Amy Kates, co-author with Jay Galbraith, of Designing Dynamic Organizations*

This book will serve as a helpful resource to employees in the midst of experiencing career transitions or organizational shifts. Richard McKnight provides a practical guide in helping employees navigate through change by ensuring they become stronger, more confident and purposeful.

—*Sally W. Stetson, Co-Founder & Principal, Salveson Stetson Group, Inc.*

This is an insightful look at the behaviors that cause individuals to succeed or fail in the face of organizational change. Dr. McKnight clearly understands both the personal and organizational dynamics of change.

—*Thomas Hoffman, former CFO, Sunoco*

This book is an easy read and I will recommend it to my career transition clients. Most people facing involuntary career transition take on what Richard McKnight calls the Victim or Survivor modes. With this book, we at last have a way of labeling those ineffective responses and, more importantly, have a constructive alternative: the way of the Navigator.

—*Anne Dunn, DBM, global outplacement and coaching firm*

As the head of HR for my company, I am constantly faced with helping others through organizational change. Richard McKnight's non-technical model of Victim, Survivor and Navigator does a fabulous job reminding us that our approach to change is a choice. He offers practical examples and tools to help identify where we are, where need to be and how to get there. I highly recommend this book.

—*Katy Theroux, SVP, HR, GS1 US*

This book is essential reading for everyone going through organizational and change. It emphasizes how we can use change as an opportunity to improve our lives. It is insightful, well written and above all practical in showing how to break out of a "victim" mentality and take charge of our own future.

—*Teresa Gavigan, Vice President, HR, Sunoco*

After coaching thousands of employees through career transition and organizational change, I'm recommending this book to both clients and friends. Richard McKnight's unique insights into how to navigate organizational change will help everyone who wants to succeed in these challenging times.

—*Connie Bowes, Vice President and Career Consultant, Lee Hecht Harrison*

This book provides the reader with an insightful roadmap on how to navigate through change, and imparts strategies for understanding and taking control of change. This book is a valuable tool for anyone who is looking to successfully navigate through the changes that are around every turn.

—*Kathy Korsen, HR Strategic Partner, Merck and Co.*

Richard McKnight helps us choose to understand ourselves and to lead a more productive and purposeful life. This book should be read by every college student and by every working adult.

—*Barbara Guido, Human Resources Consultant*

Disruptive workplace changes are a given; our reaction to those disruptions is a personal choice. Many have written on this subject but none with such eloquence, sensitivity and clarity as Richard McKnight. This is a quick read that will stay with you for a lifetime.

—*Hadley Williams, Ph.D. MBA, Managing Director, Human Productivity, LLC*

The content is accessible. Vivid examples and sound suggestions abound. You see this vital content through the eyes of everyday human beings. It is a practical guide to support your own highly personal journey. As someone who has read and studied countless books on change, I recommend it strongly.

—*Paul Hilt, President, Hilt & Associates*

This book distills 30 years of experience helping others manage personal transition in the midst of organizational change and delivers valuable insight, perspective and tips in a friendly and accessible way. This book is an important read for anyone wanting better personal outcomes from changes in their environment.

—*Mario DiCioccio, Executive Coach in private practice*

Richard McKnight has written a powerful prescription for self-management that will help all who are involved in workplace change. This book will show you how to commit to emotional and physical health and control your negative impulses while change unfolds.

—*James P. (Pat) Carlisle, President, The de Bono Group, LLC*

I highly recommend this work to anyone affected by the current economic turmoil and to those who wish to engage in their lives with a sense of purpose and possibility. Dr. McKnight's important book on individual and organizational change leads readers toward choosing their own path through life. This highly practical text provides much needed guidance through uncertain times in the workplace and economy.

—*Stephen Allan, PhD, CEO, Options Counseling Services*

Acknowledgements

You really find out who your friends are when you write your first book. Thanks to these wonderful people for suffering through a mountain of grammatical problems and for offering exceptionally valuable suggestions for making the book useful and interesting. They are Navigators, all. Thank you to the following people: Shannon Breuer, Pat Carlisle, Kim Gaber, Tom Kaney, Jennifer Loucek, Kelli McKnight, Gary Merkin, Kathy Smith, Dick Watson, Hadley Williams, Allen Zaklad. Thank you to Candace York for making it beautiful!

And special thanks to my beautiful, exceptionally insightful wife, Debbie.

Dedication

For over 20 years at irregular intervals, I have received phone calls or emails from people who heard me speak about the ideas in this book many years before. A woman in New England, for example, wrote to say that she had formed a support group at her workplace to discuss with others how to stay in Navigator mode and wanted me to know she still values the ideas after eight years. Another person called from Texas to say that after 20 years, she still tries to function as a Navigator. A person who had retired and was going through some old files found a workbook on these ideas from a course I taught in 1988 and wondered if I had ever written this book. She said the ideas helped her deal bravely with a bout of cancer.

And then there was the time I was seated on a plane next to a man who discovered I was the person who had introduced him to the Victim, Survivor, Navigator formulation. His eyes grew wide and he took my hand in both of his. "You are the man who saved my life," he said. "I truly mean it. You enabled me to get into Navigator mode."

This book is dedicated to all these lovely people and the thousands more who have been introduced to these ideas and who, until now, have been forced by my procrastination to rely only on their memories of these ideas.

Chapter 1

Stress in the Workplace

*He who has a why can
endure almost any how.*
—*Friedrich Nietzsche*

The message on the bumper sticker was stark and jarring, the un-adorned voice of the Victim: "On my way to work. Please kill me."

Wondering about the person who would put such a statement on her vehicle, a car she presumably drives to work, I crept up at the next light to have a look. She looked stressed: tousled hair, heavily furrowed brows, down-turned mouth. "At least she has a job," I thought as I drove off.

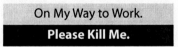

I've been hearing a lot of negative statements about work these days. For instance, one man said to me recently, "In every other house on my street is a person out of work. In each of the other houses is someone going crazy trying to do the work of those who have been laid off." While this might be the exaggeration of a defeatist, work life has become increasingly unstable and the defeatists seem to be multiplying.

"'Change-Of-The-Month Club,' I call it," another said to me. Asked to elaborate, he said, "I can't wait to see what horrors are in store for us next month. Last month they gave me a 'promotion' to a job I didn't want. Now they've asked me to fire my old associates." Change like this, I thought—or even the threat of it—can challenge the emotional wellbeing of the most resilient person.

In each of these cases, I wondered what these people might say if they actually lost the job they apparently hate. It's not that I think they should be grateful for a stressful job or value an employer who treats them poorly, but if you think having stress at work is hard, try having the stress of no work.

Some Personal Credentials

I know what it's like to lose a job. I've been there. It hurts. And makes you mad. And causes intense anxiety.

But losing a job can also be one of the most liberating experiences you could ever have. I know this from personal experience, too, and from my career-counseling colleagues who tell me this is the response of at least a third of those they coach after job loss.

I will never put a bumper sticker like that woman's on my car no matter how bad any future employment might be. True, workplaces can be unfair, humiliating, and worse. But no one is holding a gun to anyone's head to stay employed.

I am writing this in the spring of 2009, six months after the "Great Collapse" of the housing and financial markets of August 2008.

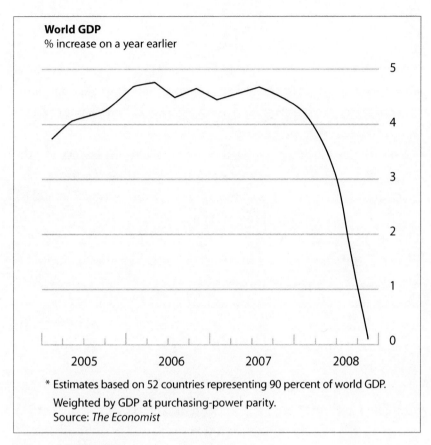

Figure 1 World GDP

Figure 1 is a rather bleak chart showing the results of the current economic problems on the growth of the World Gross Domestic Product. The WGDP, as you probably know, is the sum total of goods and services produced all over the world. As a financial executive friend of mine put it, you don't really want to see the growth of the World GDP take a nosedive like this. By the time you read this, perhaps the crisis has corrected. But even if it has, your workplace is probably still in turmoil and the leaders are trying to make it more competitive in the new, do-more-with-less economy.

High Stress in America

Let's peer into the lives of ordinary working Americans to see how workplace change is affecting them and how they're going about managing that stress. That woman with the "Please kill me" bumper sticker, it seems, has a lot of company.

Let's do this for two reasons: in comparing your experience to others, you might find yourself comforted by the fact that, if you are challenged by workplace and economic conditions, you aren't alone; and by examining the stress management habits of others, we can learn both what works and what doesn't.

As our "spy glass" into the stress managing habits of Americans, we will use data from the American Psychological Association's 2008 *Stress in America* study. This annual study (which you can read for yourself online) measures sources of stress, behaviors used to manage stress, and the impact of stress on the lives of Americans. Over 4,000 adults participated in the study in all parts of the country.

According to this study, half of Americans reported that their stress level increased over the past year, with 30 percent rating their stress level as "extreme." This continued a trend reported in 2007 when half of Americans reported that their stress had increased over the previous five years.

Stress clearly is taking a toll on people and, according to the APA, is causing or contributing to health problems, poor relationships, and lost productivity at work.

What's causing all this stress? Three things: money, the economy, and work. For over 80 percent of us, these are the chief concerns. Americans report that work is a stressor (67 percent) and that health problems in the family (67 percent) and housing costs (62 percent) are also troubling them. Job stability is a problem for over half of Americans (56 percent).

Who is struggling most: men or women? It appears that women are.

Women, for example, report that they are more stressed about money (83 percent for women, 78 percent for men), the economy (84 percent vs. 74 percent), housing costs (66 percent vs. 58 percent), and health problems affecting their families (70 percent vs. 63 percent). Women also report more symptoms of a physical and emotional nature than men do and they cope with it differently than men do. We'll come back to this below.

Let me say that again in case, like me, you get a little glazed over with a lot of statistics:

> *More than half of Americans say they are frequently troubled these days by feelings of irritability, fatigue, insomnia, and depression due to work and workplace issues!*

So how are we coping with all that stress? Well, for one thing, despite knowing we should do so, less than half of us are exercising to alleviate stress. This figure (at 47 percent) is down over the past year. We're more stressed now and we're doing less to take care of ourselves. In case you are one of the few people in the United States who has not heard this, exercise, merely taking a daily walk, can be tremendously beneficial in managing stress.

When asked what they do to cope with stress, many people mentioned the following: smoking, gambling, shopping, and drinking. Obviously, these are faulty mechanisms, at best, for dealing with stress. More disturbing yet was the percentage of people who actually believe that these behaviors are really beneficial in managing stress: 40 percent of people who smoke, for example, think so and 41 percent of the people who gamble think so.

Thankfully, the percentages of people who employ these practices in managing stress are relatively low. But of the 14 most commonly mentioned stress managing practices used by the study group,

Stress Managing Practice	Percent of Respondents
Listen to music	52%
Exercise or walk	47%
Read	44%
Spend time with friends or family	41%
Watch TV or movies for more than two hours a day	41%
Napping	38%
Play video games, surf the Internet	37%
Pray	37%
Eat	34%
Spend time on a hobby	30%
Go to church or religious services	21%
Drink alcohol	18%
Shop	18%
Smoke	16%

Figure 2 What Americans are doing to manage stress

seven—including the questionable practices mentioned above, are offered as preferred techniques. I've darkened the most questionable techniques (see Figure 2).

All of those in the tinted rows, above, are either forms of escape or self-soothing techniques. None will really help you cope well with stress. But back to male-female differences. Figure 3 shows some other comparisons.

	Percent of respondents	
	Women	Men
Eating to manage stress	39%	29%
Drinking to manage stress	15%	22%
Doing enough to manage stress (said yes)	50%	39%
Experience headaches	56%	36%
Feel depressed or sad	56%	39%
Feel as though could cry	55%	23%

Figure 3 Coping mechanisms employed by men and women

Finally, perhaps the most disturbing finding of all is that while Americans are clearly troubled by workplace and economic issues, and while a majority of Americans are willing to share their troubles with their spouses as a means of dealing with stress, nearly half of Americans say they would be uncomfortable asking someone they know for help in managing stress. Almost six in 10 would be very reluctant to reach out for professional advice to manage the problems stress is creating in their lives. As you will read later, doing so is good stress management. It's not a sign of weakness to reach out for help; it's a sign of strength.

Most Employees are Disengaged

Now, let's get in the car with the woman who's traveling to work with that "Please kill me" sticker on her bumper. What might we find at her workplace? We know she's not the only one who's struggling these days.

For an answer, we might look to the results of a study of employee engagement conducted in the fall of 2008 by the Corporate Executive Board. It describes four disturbing trends:

1. *At the very time our economy needs high levels of productivity, employee performance is declining dramatically.*

   According to this report, the number of employees offering their employers high levels of discretionary effort has decreased by 53 percent since 2005. Discretionary effort is the energy an employee might put forth in helping a coworker solve a problem, the extra hours devoted to helping a client, or the decision to polish an important presentation one more time.

2. *Senior leader effort has declined dramatically.*

   Disengagement is showing up at all levels: in 2008 only 13 percent of senior executives reported that they put forth high levels of discretionary effort compared to 29 percent in the second half of 2006.

3. *Disengaged employees are digging in.*

   Disengaged employees, who are less productive than engaged employees, are significantly less likely to quit in now than in years past.

4. *The most talented and valuable employees want to leave.*

   According to this report 25 percent of a company's most valued talent intends to quit in the next 12 months.

To me, these statistics reveal that many employees are living in a state of quiet desperation: they're disaffected by work, but they aren't saying anything about it. And many of their leaders, at least metaphorically, are sitting in the parking lot with their motors running, just waiting for the recession to end.

Three Choices

As an organizational consultant for over many years, I have had the opportunity to observe literally thousands of employees as they've been forced to cope with sweeping organizational change. During that time, I have worked with over 100 organizations that were in transition. I have advised executives as they've made widespread changes in organizational structure, business processes, and reward systems. I have helped them break the news of these changes to employees and I have helped the employees in those organizations deal with the psychological impact of their decisions.

As part of that work, I have discovered that there are three fundamental ways of responding to change of any sort, whether on- or off-the-job. These choices are usually made unconsciously and have radically different consequences. Over the course of my career, I have conducted hundreds of workshops designed to help employees stay productive during change. In each of those seminars, I have articulated those three choices.

One of the three choices—to play the Victim—is ineffective in managing the stress of organizational change. Another—the Survivor mode—is more effective than the Victim mode is but it, too, leaves a lot to be desired. The remaining response works exceptionally well. I call it the Navigator mode. To adopt this approach means not only that you are more likely to enjoy greater workplace satisfaction but also to have increased satisfaction with your life in general. In every workplace a percentage of people employ the Navigator response, those who make the best of change. They continue to grow and develop despite the difficulties surrounding them. You will learn about those employees here and I will encourage you to emulate them partly because they suffer less from the stress of change than their coworkers.

You will learn through this book that during change being a Victim, a Survivor, or a Navigator. It's up to you. You will learn that being a negative and reactive Victim carries with it potentially severe negative repercussions. You will learn that while most people respond to change by making the Survivor's choice, opting for it will eventually leave you unfulfilled, stressed-out, and possibly depressed. Finally, you will learn that if you really want to be the master of your own fate and make the best of workplace change, you'll have to create your own North Star and function like what I call a Navigator.

In the typical organization, change begins when senior executives decide change is necessary. They're like battlefield generals. The generals see a need for change and then tell others—usually middle managers—to carry out the orders. I think of middle-level managers as "strategy lieutenants." They salute the generals smartly and do their best to implement the change their superiors have said is necessary. Finally, there is everyone else, the vast bulk of employees whom I call the "cannon fodder" of change because they're farthest from the decision-making and often have to pay the highest personal toll when change unfolds.

I have written this book to offer all three groups a constructive path. If you live at the bottom of your organization, you need to function as a Navigator because it's the best way to take care of yourself. But you also want and need your leaders to function as Navigators because when leaders function like Victims or Survivors they create a lot of misery for people below them.

Some readers of this book may be in transition, i.e., between jobs. This book can help you, too even though most of the examples relate to ongoing work circumstances. If you are in the midst of a career search, you need the counsel in this book at least as much as other readers who are currently employed because successful job transition will require you to manage stress exceptionally well.

How the Book is Organized

Chapter Two, "Perception and Reality," tells you how your perceptions about yourself and your world can determine your fate and how they lead to the three responses to change.

Chapters Three through Five describe those choices in detail. Chapter Six offers tips, guidelines, and practical suggestions to enable you to get yourself in Navigator mode during change. Finally, Chapter Seven has exercises, checklists, and worksheets to help you determine who you are at work right now, how workplace change is affecting you, and how you can make the best of your situation.

Since this book is written for employees undergoing organizational change, the examples given will focus primarily on work life, but the ideas and guidelines offered here generally apply regardless of the kind of change you are facing. I wish you the best as you go through the adventure of change, whatever it may be.

On page 90 is a simple questionnaire. It will give you some feedback about the extent to which your current outlook parallels that of the Victim, Survivor, or Navigator. You can fill it out now or wait until you've read the entire book to take it. Whether you dive in now or later please be clear: this questionnaire is not a diagnostic "test." It is not intended to slap a label on you or anyone else. You will learn by reading this book that no one is purely a Victim, only a Survivor, or exclusively a Navigator. The value of the instrument will be in using your scores to deepen your understanding about the Victim, Survivor, and Navigator ways of thinking and using the insights you gain to fashion a constructive response to your own situation.

Finally, consider visiting my website. It contains a rich array of resources devoted to helping you understand and stay in Navigator mode. The site offers an short essays describing remarkable people who function as Navigators, excerpts from other books I've written, and an art gallery. Finally, on this site are guided meditation podcasts that will help you relax, meditate, and focus on your goals in a powerful way.

Happy reading and stay on course!

Chapter 2

Perception and Reality

*There is nothing good nor
bad but thinking makes it so.*
—*William Shakespeare*

Once I read a good book about the accelerating rate of change.
The author urgently warned that the pace of change was overtaking
our human ability to cope. "Change," he wrote, "is avalanching on
our heads and we are grotesquely unprepared to deal with it." It was
Alvin Toffler—in 1969—in the book *Future Shock*. Toffler defined
future shock as "the dizzying disorientation caused by the premature
arrival of the future." While Toffler was right to be concerned about
the pace of change, it has only accelerated since the late 1960s!

Forty years later, I recalled that book as I passed by a newsstand
and I gave myself a challenge: write a headline that captures today's
challenges with respect to workplace change. I settled on this one:
"EVERYTHING IS UP FOR GRABS!" There is much evidence

showing that work is stressful for everyone lately, from the top of the organization to the bottom.

One executive, for example, described his plight to me recently by saying, "To stay alive in this economy, we have to make radical changes in our operating structure. This is just to *keep up* with our competitors, not to get ahead. And we believe we have to do it in just 90 days. We'll make mistakes, but we have no choice."

I asked him: "What is the implication of this for the employees in your organization?"

"Simple," he said. "These days, at this company, you don't want to be an ordinary employee with ordinary capabilities in dealing with change. If you are, you're going to be miserable at best."

Vulnerability and Hardiness

Everyone perceives and reacts to change differently. Psychologists know that when predicting a person's response to change it is more important to know who the person is than what the specific circumstances are: some will perceive change to be a welcome challenge or opportunity while others will believe a disaster is at hand. And both parties will be "right."

Generally, if our world is changing, but we perceive ourselves to be in a situation over which we have mastery, we will experience little stress. I use the term *hardy* to refer to this state of mind. The dictionary defines "hardy" as "having or manifesting great force or power." When we're hardy, we feel energetic, optimistic, robust, and masterful.

On the other hand, when stressed, we perceive our world to be in turmoil and we doubt our ability to cope. We feel vulnerable. We feel exposed, susceptible, out of control, and at the mercy of events.

The conditions leading to vulnerability then, are as follows:

Vulnerability, Condition 1:

We experience our work situation as threatening to our well-being.

Vulnerability Condition, 2:

We believe that we cannot or probably cannot cope adequately with these changes.

Vulnerability may be expressed in a formula:

Vulnerability = Perceived Threat + Perceived Inability To Cope With The Threat

The key word in this definition is "perceived." How we perceive our world and assess our ability to cope with it will determine our responses to the situation. Even though two employees may get the same memo describing a merger or reorganization, they may have very different reactions to it: their unique understanding of the situation, combined with their appraisal of their ability to cope with it, determine their responses.

Conversely, when we experience ourselves as hardy, the following conditions are true:

Hardiness Condition 1:

We perceive our situation to be changing in a way that is challenging (vs. threatening or problematic).

Hardiness Condition 2:

We perceive ourselves to be capable of rising to the challenge.

Hardiness = Perceived Challenge + Perceived Personal Competence

Three Ways Of Self-Managing

In Figure 4, you will see the terms we discussed above: "vulnerable" and "hardy." These are related to the concept of "perceived personal power," also on the left of the line. This shows in graphic form that our perceptions of our situation and ourselves determine how vulnerable or hardy we are.

When we perceive ourselves as having little personal power, three increasingly self-defeating things happen. If we're feeling especially pessimistic and powerless, a fourth consequence follows:

+ We think self-defeating thoughts about ourselves and the situation such as, "I'm in trouble," "I'm getting used," "I'll never be able to get him to listen to my ideas," "I can't impact the direction of this project," and the like.

+ We experience an uncomfortable set of feelings that flow from these thoughts—disappointment, dread, fear, rage, hatred, anxiety, and/or depression.

+ We engage in short-term, emergency-oriented behaviors that are designed to quell the uncomfortable feelings we are having.

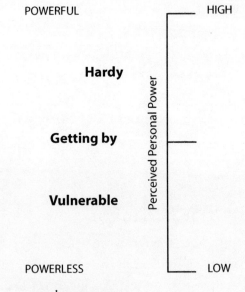

Figure 4 Three personal assessments

• If we feel stressed enough, we tend to engage in risky, "what the hell" behaviors that under normal circumstances we would never consider, e.g., shouting at a boss or coworker, walking off the job in a huff, resorting to drugs for relief, or worse.

According to recent research, a mutually reinforcing feedback loop sets up in the brain under severe stress: first, stress causes the release of powerful hormones that increase fear and inhibit aggression. The resulting aggression—sometimes turned on oneself—triggers the release of additional stress hormones. That's why the frustration of a traffic jam can lead to full-blown road rage and why it's so hard, at times, to calm oneself after a stressful event: the more stress accumulates, the stronger our reactions become and the more agitated we feel.

The good news is that we can learn to cultivate a response that goes the other direction. If we can maintain some semblance of self-confidence in a situation, three good things subsequently happen, each of which is increasingly self-empowering:

• We think self-esteem-enhancing thoughts about ourselves and the situation such as, "I've handled more than this before," "I know I can contribute to this project," "This gives me the encouragement I need to try new skills," "This is a challenge, not a problem," and the like.

• As a result, we produce within ourselves a feeling or set of feelings that generate energy, enthusiasm, curiosity, exploration, and alertness.

• We engage in a set of behaviors aimed at taking advantage of the opportunities.

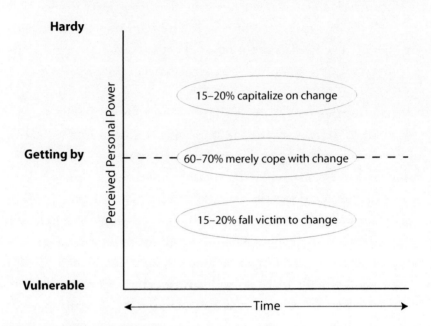

Figure 5 Effects of workplace change

As you can see in Figure 5, a typical workplace population will distribute into three basic categories. Fifteen–twenty percent will fall victim to change, 60–70 percent will scrape by, and 15–20 percent will capitalize on it.

Psychologists use the term "locus-of-control," to refer to an individual's perception about where the power is located in his or her life. There are essentially two possibilities: it's inside the person— *internal* locus-of-control—or it's outside of him or her—*external* locus-of-control.

It works like this: if I have an *internal* locus-of-control, I perceive that I am the cause of rather than at the effect of events. When good things happen in my life, I tend to believe I did a lot to make those things happen. When bad things happen, I tend to believe that I can do what's necessary to make the best of the situation.

The reverse is true if I have an *external* locus-of-control: I am more likely to believe that forces outside myself (people, luck, fate) are against me and that I probably can't do much to minimize or capitalize on those events. Research in a variety of fields has made clear that to the extent to which your locus-of-control is *inside* you, you will tend to be more successful in sports, in romance, in business settings, and, indeed, will enjoy many more of life's benefits than those whose locus-of-control is external. Even your physical health will benefit.

Figure 6 applies the terms Victim, Survivor, and that flow from our perception of ourselves and our circumstances. The up and down lines are meant to show that life is a process with its ups and downs: even the most committed defeatist occasionally feels moments of personal power, and even the self-confident Navigator has periods of self-doubt.

At the bottom of the chart is the realm of the "*Victim.*" We function as Victims when we perceive ourselves as threatened with a situation we cannot or probably will not be able to handle. When we're

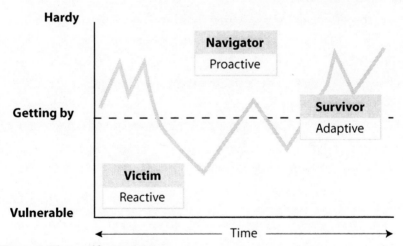

Figure 6 Three self-assessments

in the Victim-mode, we employ inadequate coping mechanisms, in turn adding to our own powerlessness. The vicious cycle becomes a self-fulfilling prophecy. To the extent that we expect trouble and disappointment, we will look for it, and not surprisingly, we will find it. We are "reactive."

"*Survivor*" behavior, in the middle of the chart, results when we perceive ourselves as capable of living through adversity but fear that we'll do little more than that. Many people pride themselves on being able to "hang in there," while proudly announcing, "I am a survivor!" However, when they do so, they run the risk of burning out from the grasping and clinging they can convince themselves is necessary. Many of us fortify ourselves with the belief that while we can't change our circumstances, we must cling tenaciously to what we have. We try to adjust ourselves to events; we're "adaptive."

There are two main "flavors" of Survivor mode, each of which is very visible during organizational change: *Pleasers* who do and say what is needed to gain approval and *Warriors* who compete, demand, and confront. I describe these varieties in Chapter Four, "The Survivor Response."

At the top of the chart is the realm of the "*Navigator.*" We function like a Navigator when we believe in our ability to deal competently with our situation and display effective, reality-based coping behavior, focused energy, and assertiveness. This is, by far, the most effective approach to managing change. In Navigator mode, we are not reactive or merely adaptive; we are "proactive," finding ways to turn change to our advantage.

Let's look at each mode in turn.

Chapter 3

The Victim Response

Wherever I go, I go, too—and spoil everything.
—Samuel Hoffenstein

If I perceive myself to be powerless in a threatening situation, I will almost certainly react as a Victim. If I do so, I will either fight or take flight.

Here is what we know about the fight/flight syndrome: it is the most extreme response to stress. It's the body's more or less automatic response to severe threat, no matter the form that threat takes. For example, if we're faced with the threat of attack by a dangerous animal, subjected to prolonged, excessive noise, or extremes of heat or cold—all physical stressors—our bodies will go into fight/flight mode. The sole aim of fight/flight is shortsighted and urgent: to reduce the threat by taking dramatic action. If we shout at another driver who comes close to hitting our car, or slam down the phone because we've been kept on hold for too long, we are engaging in fight behavior. If we abruptly quit our job because we're distressed by it, we are engaging in flight behavior. Drinking, eating, or sleeping too much is flight behavior, as well.

Whether the source of stress is physical or psychological we will go into fight/flight mode if we experience the event as threatening. For instance, in the face of family strife, the death of a loved one, or decline in our financial status, most people will activate the fight/flight response to some degree. But this is not certain and the level of activation isn't, either. It turns out that in the interval between stressful event and behavioral reaction, we insert a psychological response that either aggravates or minimizes the intensity of our fight-flight response. At some level, how we respond, if not exactly a choice, is subject to alteration.

When hearing me talk about these matters, I've heard people defensively say things like, "Any red-blooded person is going to feel stressed if they lose a job." I've come to learn that this is a disguised way of noting that in some cases employees truly are the victims of poor decisions made by others. I quickly acknowledge that agreeing to work for any organization means that we put ourselves at the consequences of others' decisions, not all of which are going to benefit us. But after working with thousands of people who were being laid off, I am more convinced than ever that the *meaning* of job stress is self-determined. In other words, job loss may or may not be perceived as a threat—it depends on who is losing the job.

Some people, when receiving a pink slip, are enormously relieved. Others are glad it happened because they're now free to move on to other career pursuits. And yes, others—most others—feel seriously threatened and anxious. The key, again, is personal perception. To the extent to which we perceive ourselves as powerless, job loss will be as hazardous to us as if it were a physical threat. And the resulting action will be selected from a very short list of options: fight or flight.

Victim Mode: The Easiest Response

During the early phases of dramatic and unexpected change, many of us will behave like the Victim at least temporarily, especially if the nature of the change is sudden. Doing so is a common response to the shock of change.

A few months ago, I saw this close at hand while working with a very large group of employees who were told that their jobs would end in 10-12 months. The setting was a small mid-western town where their company was the largest employer. Most of the employees had lived all their lives in that community but came to realize that when their company shut down, they would most likely have to move away to find other employment. I arrived on the scene just days after the announcement. The most common manifestation of the shock was denial, a form of flight. Despite declarations that the company was closing— made by the CEO, the Governor of the state, and the Mayor of the town—I repeatedly heard people say things like, "I think the company can still pull this out" and "Until I see a pink slip, I won't believe this is actually happening."

When in Victim mode, the darkly comical slogan, "Life's a bitch, and then you die" can have vivid meaning. The Victim mindset, revealed by this expression, is one of inadequacy and scarcity: our experience of the world, at least at that moment, is one of insufficiency. We perceive that the difficulties are just beginning and that our troubles are due to "THEM," that is, unnamed authority figures. We experience ourselves as oppressed, at risk of being oppressed further, and able to do little or nothing to prevent the troubles that will surely come.

Because we tend to expect the worst when we are in the Victim state, our energy drains away in downward-spiraling defeatist thoughts. A vicious cycle sets in: first we experience anxiety, then physical tension, then worsening anxiety. Energy that might have been used to understand and cope artfully with our situation becomes scattered in fruitless preoccupation: others have let us down, horrible things might happen, and so on.

Fight and Flight Behavior

Although most of us prefer one form to the other, when we feel victimized, we often respond by flipping quickly back and forth between fight and flight responses. Look at these lists: which behaviors do you tend to employ when you're at your worst?

Fight Behavior

Becoming negative and resistant

Expressing hostility

Blaming or attacking others

Threatening to or actually sabotaging production or quality

Employing sarcastic humor about the change or those initiating the change

Complaining

Procrastinating

Being uncooperative

Flight Behavior

Escaping (through TV watching, eating, alcohol, drugs, or other escapes)

Sleeping or eating too much

Getting sick

Pretending to be sick

Giving up

Showing up late and/or leaving early

Idealizing the way things used to be

While it's always easiest to spot Victim behavior when it shows up in pure form as a fight or flight behavior, it can take a hybrid form too, by way of what psychologists call passive-aggression. Passive-aggression is a combination of fight and flight behavior. Common manifestations of passive-aggressive action are work slow-downs, grumbling, saying, "It's not in my job description," product tampering, damaging equipment, and stealing from the company. It can also take creative and particularly destructive forms. For instance, just before a layoff, an employee at a healthcare information company replaced every occurrence in the database of the word "cancer" with his boss' name, and every occurrence of the word "disease" with the name of the Chairman of the Board. It took the company months to eradicate the mischief.

When we operate from a Victim mindset, our ability to cope with change is diminished. To be a Victim is to perceive that we are in the midst of an emergency. We feel threatened, personally wronged, and justified in considering drastic short-term measures to protect ourselves.

The Voice of the Victim

Below are actual statements I've heard people make during workplace change. They reflect the vulnerability and cynicism of the Victim response.

> "The little guy is going to get screwed."

> "Only the game players will get ahead."

> "It's all politics."

> "Nothing is going to happen. They're just trying to shake us up."

> "I'll put in a lot of extra work and then I'll get fired."

"They say they care about us, but they really only care about profit."

Office humor often expresses the voice of the Victim. I once saw a cartoon at a company where layoffs were occurring that showed a particularly inept magician attempting the trick in which the lady in the box appears to be sawed in two. Only in the cartoon, the lady was really being bisected! The two halves of the box were hand-labeled with the company name and with the name of the division that was being divested. Over the magician's face was pasted a photo of the chairman of the board of the divesting company.

Here is dark joke that typifies the Victim mentality, attributed to Harry Truman:

If your neighbor gets laid off it's a recession.

If your spouse gets laid off it's a depression.

If you get laid off it's a disaster.

Sometimes it's easier to deal with uncomfortable feelings through humor, but those who employ this kind of humor rarely get in touch with the feelings that underlie it. Sarcasm is a hallmark of the Victim mode.

When we're in Victim mode and complaining, what are we so upset about? Research reveals that most specific sources of on-the-job stress fall into one of three categories: overload, i.e., having too much to do and not enough time, ambiguity, i.e., lacking the information you need to do your job well (or to know if your job will continue!), and conflict, i.e., either strife with coworkers or ethical conflict. There is another category of job stress that is less specific yet more taxing: lack of control over our circumstances. If we feel bad things are about to happen and we feel ourselves to be unable to prevent those things, most people go into Victim mode quickly and deeply.

Many years ago, researchers wanted to know which monkey suffered the most from stress: a monkey who had the ability to control an apparatus that prevented a shock—the "executive" monkey—or the one paired with the executive monkey who could only watch and hope the executive monkey would make the right decision. Nearly every time, both the executive monkey, the one that could terminate the electric shock, and the passive monkey suffered from stress.

Dependency

When we're in Victim-mode, we perceive our future to be in the hands of others. We perceive ourselves to be needy and beholden. But the truth is, no one above us, below us, or at our level can guarantee our future—or destroy it for that matter.

When we feel dependent and victimized, we can become very angry at the authorities that we perceive to be letting us down. At times like this we can feel justified in engaging in very self-serving behavior. Such behavior rises dramatically when we believe that others cannot be trusted. We tend to feel distrustful when we perceive ourselves to be at the mercy of another person—which often occurs during change.

Again, one might reasonably ask: "Since we're often at the mercy of others during organizational change, isn't it natural to feel anxious at such times?" The answer is YES! Anxiety during change, especially when the nature of that change is ambiguous, is perfectly normal and natural. The task is to acknowledge these feelings and to choose the most constructive response. Those who study resilience under stress say that acknowledging how we feel is the first step in choosing our response. When we're in Victim mode, we are neither self-aware nor deliberate. Instead, we've reactive.

It's important to realize that the Victim response is not limited to those at the bottom of the hierarchy. Any of us can fall into Victim mode, regardless of our status. Richard Nixon was one of America's most famous Victims. On being defeated in an election once, in classic Victim fashion, he said to reporters, "Well, you won't have Nixon to kick around any more."

If responding like a Victim is so ineffective, why do so many of us manage to produce feelings of hopelessness or cynicism during change? Partly, because Victim responses were learned when we were kids. We learn Victim behaviors early in life when we really *are* powerless. And partly, we act like Victims because it's "in the wiring." We have a nervous system that, for better or worse, is error-activated: like Mallard ducks and garter snakes, we are programmed to take dramatic action to preserve our safety, especially when things feel unpredictable and chaotic. The bigger and more threatening the change, the more likely our error-activated nature will be stimulated.

We also choose the way of the Victim because for all its drawbacks, it simplifies complexity and minimizes our sense of personal responsibility. If I can blame others for my troubles, if I can convince myself that I only have one choice in how I behave, my world feels more predictable, and somehow, I feel better—at least for the moment.

Finally, when we fall into the behavior of the Victim we join with others who see the world the way we do. It's a psychological place that, at least temporarily, feels safe and even warranted: misery, as the popular expression goes, loves company.

The Future Determines the Present

Key to understanding the Victim response lies in comprehending what the Victim mind believes the future holds: trouble. When we fall into Victim mode, we believe we are in peril.

This brings to mind an expression, "the future determines the present," which refers to the awesome power of our expectations to

Figure 7 The young lady/old lady

actually create the future we expect. A classic example is the bank rush of the late 1920s. Expecting their banks to fail, many bank patrons, by rushing to withdraw their money, indeed caused those banks to fail. The anticipated future—bank collapse—was brought about by the feared result.

We're contemplating the matter of perception, the psychological process of making sense of data taken in by our senses. Figure 7 shows a well-known optical illusion that vividly illustrates how perception can markedly affect what we perceive. Some people look at this and see a young lady, some see an old lady. Don't concern yourself with which image you saw first: this is not a psychological test!

This picture was used in a famous psychological experiment. Here is how it worked: half the subjects in the study were given a short lecture on the challenges of being an elderly woman in today's world. Afterwards, they were shown this picture. Over 70 per cent of these subjects said the picture was that of an old lady. The other half of the

29

subjects was given a lecture on the challenges of being a young woman in today's world, and then was shown the picture. They saw the young lady in almost equal measure.

While this illustration reveals the power of expectation on perception, the phenomenon of expectation determines much more than what we see. Our expectations markedly affect our thinking, our feelings, and critically, our behavior. When we expect a particular outcome or result, we tend to create the conditions that bring it about. The psychological literature is filled with studies that bear this out and because the tendency is so strong, the field of medical research rigorously controls for this effect.

For instance, the expectation that a medicine will benefit you and produce actual health benefits is profound. That's why in most pharmaceutical research, subjects do not know whether they are taking a placebo or the actual medicine under investigation. Further, they do not know what effect the medicine is expected to produce. This is called a "double-blind" study design.

Studies have long shown that one person's expectation of another person's future can also determine the present! For example, a series of famous studies by Robert Rosenthal and Lenore Jacobson demonstrated that the expectations of teachers could markedly affect student performance. In a controlled experiment, the researchers caused teachers to regard some children as capable of accelerated learning and others as slow to learn even though the children were randomly assigned to groups. The teachers, expecting quicker results from some students, unconsciously engaged in behavior that helped those kids learn more and faster. The teachers' expectations of the future determined their behavior in the present.

We're discussing the Victim mentality here, but there is good news associated with the self-fulfilling prophecy phenomenon: it can be beneficial as well as detrimental. In later chapters, we'll explore how people functioning in Navigator mode use expectations about the future and learn how to employ their future-creating strategies.

We operate out of a Victim mindset when we expect and look for the worst in our situation. When we do so, we fail to consider all our options. In many ways reacting like a Victim is very satisfying: we can convince ourselves that we're right and others are wrong. Being a Victim is easy, but unfortunately does not produce the stable world we want.

It is not always easy to accept that seeing ourselves as a Victim is a choice. Yet it truly is. It is a choice to expect trouble. And when we expect trouble, we tend to look for trouble. When we expect and look for trouble, we tend to find it. It's a self-fulfilling prophecy.

Occasionally, when I am introducing groups of people to these ideas, someone asks, "Do you have to go through Victim mode to become a Navigator?" The answer is no. No one has to spend any time at all in Victim mode. But most of us do. Be patient with yourself if you find yourself here. At times, others ask, "How do you get yourself out of Victim mode when you're in it? I find it difficult to do so." The short answer is this: practice. Our ability to choose how we react is a function of our habits. The more you catch yourself in the act of thinking and acting like the Victim and choose to stop, the easier it gets. In Chapter Six I provide detailed guidance for cultivating these habits.

Chapter 4

The Survivor Response

> *Remembering that you are going to die is the*
> *best way I know to avoid the trap of thinking*
> *you have something to lose. You are already naked.*
> *There is no reason not to follow your heart.*
> —Steve Jobs, Commencement Address Remarks

If acting like a Victim is the easiest thing to do during change, responding like the Survivor is the next easiest response—and by far the most common. The behaviors associated with the Survivor mode are usually watered-down versions of the fight/flight Victim behaviors. You might think of them as fight or flight behaviors overlaid with a veneer of social appropriateness.

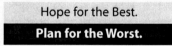

The response is widespread because when we function like a Survivor, we are doing what many of us were taught from very early in life: to employ caution and proceed warily. Survivor mode is the result of years of conditioning. To illustrate the point, below is a list of things parents commonly teach their children. To a degree, each of these teachings can assist us, but to an equal degree, they will get in our way when we want to grow from the Survivor mindset to the Navigator way of thinking.

"If you can't say something nice, don't say anything at all."

"The best defense is a good offense."

"You have to go along to get along."

"Don't let anyone push you around. When you know you are right there is no reason to listen to anyone else."

While the Victim mode involves dramatically fleeing from the situation that is causing stress or reacting angrily, as Survivors, we employ a more moderate reaction. When we function in the Survivor mode, it's as if our parents were whispering caution in our ear. If our parents were more flight-oriented, they might have encouraged us to "Be nice," or to "Go along." If they were more fight-oriented, they might have said something like "Don't let anyone shove you around; maneuver around them." You may have heard one type of message from one parent, and the other type from your other parent.

When our parents spoke to us in these ways, they were offering us—as small children—their best judgment about how to get along in the world. Unfortunately, parental advice, like any other kind of advice, is based on generalities that don't always apply to the specific situations in which we find ourselves as adults and if not thrown overboard by the maturing person, can lead to a life of clinging, defending, and grabbing.

Being a Survivor is Not Bad…But…

In everyday speech, people say proudly of themselves, "Don't worry about me, I'm a survivor," or admiringly of others, "Don't worry about her, she's a survivor." It's worth asking ourselves though: Isn't there more to life than merely surviving? This is where my ears prick up: when I hear people use the term survivor in the workplace, almost always they're referring to behavioral stances and positions that arise from a forecast of a potentially negative future, and a personal hardening against that possibility.

You may have a reaction to the term "Survivor." When this term is used in medical circles or by psychotherapists who deal with the victims of abuse, being a survivor is a good thing. I am using the term very differently here. I am using it to refer to a mindset that limits our possibilities for growth during change.

There is an old story concerning a frog that demonstrates going through life like a Survivor. It is said that if you put a frog into a pan of boiling water, it will correctly conclude that it's in trouble and will jump out of the pan. On the other hand, if you put the frog into a pan of cold water, it will relax and enjoy its surroundings. If you then heat that pan of cold water very slowly, the frog will stay in the pan until it boils to death.

People, like frogs, can literally adapt themselves to death as they seek self-preservation. Part of the reason for this is as we focus on self-preservation, the energy we have for making our lives work goes down. We have a split in our expectation of the future: it could be benign; it could be disastrous. In graphic form, Figure 8 shows what this looks like.

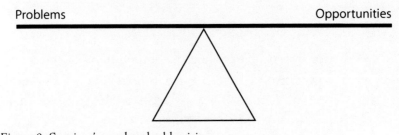

Figure 8 Survivor's employ double vision

A Commitment to Defense

The Survivor mode might be called the soldier's response because it is a commitment to defense. I recall a famous general who, when asked how a military leader prepares for a possible war, said, "We hope for the best and prepare for the worst." This might be appropriate in situations where one's goals are unclear and when any wrong move might mean catastrophe. But as a mode of living, such a stance is costly. Fundamentally, it is a state of tension and it leads to burnout. (Talk about costly: are you aware that currently the U.S. spends $1.98 billion/day on Military expenses? This is over 1/3 of the Federal budget!)

When I am speaking to groups about the Survivor mode, I ask the audience to make a tight fist with one hand. "Just clench your fist while you listen to me." I invite them to notice that while holding the tension, their focus on what I'm saying diminishes; their attention is divided between my voice and the physical sensations. I point out that if they were required at that moment to solve a complex problem but one which fell within their competence, their performance would surely be worse than if they were completely relaxed.

"Now," I tell them, "*v-e-r-y* slowly, begin to relax your grip. Just let the tension begin to slip away." I ask them to not extend their fingers once they let the tension subside: "Just let your fingers assume the position they wish to maintain. Don't extend your fingers out. Just let them do what they wish but do let the tension go."

The result amazes most people. While they have let all the voluntary tension go in their fingers, those fingers are still tightly curled. The ligaments and tendons are still carrying a good deal of tension until something is done to rid them of tension. I invite them to then slowly extend their fingers and feel the creaking resistance of their fingers to that stretching. It's a variation on that physical law: a body in tension tends to stay in tension unless something happens to alleviate it.

What's the point? If we go through our days feeling guarded and wary, we are going to introduce levels of tension in muscles, tendons, and ligaments throughout out bodies, not to mention increase levels of stress hormones. We might even get a good night's sleep, but our bodies are still harboring chronic low-level tension. We might even feel relaxed but we really aren't.

The Survivor outlook gives rise to a stress-managing style that is akin to driving down the highway with one foot on the gas and the other foot on the brake. We rev ourselves up with readiness to fight, but we slow ourselves down with caution. The car still goes, but is under great strain. Something is going to give at some point. When we are in Survivor mode for a lengthy period of time—and many of us are—what gives is often our physical health.

If you live in a state of chronic low-level tension for too long the signs of physical distress and breakdown will begin to appear. National health statistics show this. The American Academy of Family Physicians states that more than two-thirds of the visits to family doctors are for "somatoform" or "psychosomatic" disorders. These are real, physical illnesses caused by chronic, unabated stress. Obviously, a lot of us are holding on pretty tight, or at least we're trying to. And it's hurting us. We're burning out from our Survivor-oriented clinging and grasping. Many people calling on their family doctors today will complain of tension headaches, chronic lower back pain, or other illnesses aggravated by stress.

We burn out because our way of dealing with uncertainty is faulty. It seems to make a lot of sense to be committed to surviving, but this mindset doesn't work over the long haul.

Limitations of Surviving

The limitations of the Survivor mode stem from the very essence of the response. Those who are intent on merely surviving apply critical thinking processes limited only to a consideration of actions that maintain the status quo. To be a Survivor in the sense used here, we try to adapt to the way things are and thus tend to overlook new possibilities.

If we respond like a Survivor, our feelings about what is going on may be intense, but unlike the Victim who often shows less restraint, we stop ourselves from acting our feelings out directly. Instead of shouting at our boss, for example, our parental conditioning will come in to prevent it. When we hear ourselves say things like, "That kind of response can get you fired, you idiot," or "You'll be ignored or made fun of if you say what's on your mind," this is what is occurring.

If the language and thought process of the Victim reflects a perception of a dangerous, unpredictable, and hostile world, the Survivor sees a better world, but only directionally so. The world of the Survivor is not outright menacing, but is often perceived as tricky, ominous, and relatively unfriendly. Some of the articles and books for employees on how to cope with organizational change use words like "surviving" and "survival" in the titles—unwittingly contributing to a myth that fuels the Survivor mentality. These pieces suggest that organizational change is risky business and that you'd better hang on for dear life.

Over a 30-year career consulting to organizations, I've observed two predominant variations on the Survivor theme. I refer to them as the "Warriors" and the "Pleasers." Most of us tend to prefer either the Warrior or Pleaser style when in Survivor-mode.

The Warrior Mode

A common phrase maintains that, "The best defense is a good offense." This is the thinking of the Survivor, Warrior variety. Warrior mode is the psychological stance of people who have some confidence that they can hold their own in the world, *if* they act tough and take a fighting posture.

Those in Warrior mode cope with the uncertainty of organizational change by treating it like a contest they are hell-bent to win. A person falling into Warrior mode can collect and disperse information on organizational changes in a way that advantages them and disadvantages others. The problem with the Warrior's stance is that it leaves us behaviorally hardened when resilience would be more valuable and it tends to provoke others into defending themselves against us instead of supporting us.

The Warrior perceives a situation of scarcity and sets out to ensure security. When this is our perception, we can justify to ourselves engaging in behavior that others commonly refer to as "politics." In customary usage, this term simply means that one person—the one "playing politics"—tries to win at others' expense. Here are some common forms of such behavior at work:

+ Making "end runs" around others to their boss

+ Dropping names in order to win support

+ Deliberately covering up one's true views in order to buy time

+ Pitting one person against another

+ Withholding information to gain favor or minimize another's chances of success

When we respond as a Warrior, our mindset—often quite unconscious—is:

> "I am at risk of becoming a Victim. This is unthinkable. Therefore, I am going to get whatever I can, even if this means I have to muscle some weak ones out of the way. I'd be a fool not to—it's dog eat dog out there."

Illustration

I coached an executive who typified this approach to work. Let's call her Connie. Connie prided herself on being competitive. I was coaching her because while she was exceptionally bright, she was difficult to get along with. By our second or third coaching session I had heard her proudly say many times, "I'm very competitive."

"What does that mean to you, Connie?" I finally asked. I was very curious because she measured as exceptionally needy of the approval of others on the psychological tests I administered. Being competitive, one might argue, is the opposite of what such a person would rationally do to gain the veneration of others.

Connie's answer, delivered with a smug smile was, "Simple. Being competitive means I want to win."

"What does winning mean to you?" I inquired.

"Doing the very best. Being the very best," she replied.

I don't think I helped Connie much. I could never get her to see that being and doing the best did not have to mean being perfect— what I think her real goal was. Her perfectionistic mindset made her suspicious of the motives of others, thus leading her to feel justified in holding others at arm's length through her competitiveness. She was always on guard, always seeking to one-up others. These tendencies diminished her ability to problem solve creatively or benefit from collaboration. In Warrior mode, she was headed for burnout and was perpetually confused about why her peers held her at arm's length—all the while holding *them* at arm's length.

Several years ago, the Center for Creative Leadership reported on research that exposed the risk of behaviors like those we're discussing to one's career. They used the term "derailing behavior" and noted that the type of behavior I am referring to, i.e., Warrior mode, is quite likely to hold you back in most organizational settings.

A man in a recent seminar typified this view when he said, "My motto is, 'It's better to be pissed off than be pissed on'." The ironic consequence of pitting yourself against others is that doing so erodes goodwill and actually contributes to the scarcity it's supposed to protect you from. People who tend to go for the jugular when things get tense fail to build supportive relationships. Mistakenly, they view their own coiled wariness as their best friend.

The Pleaser Mode

Turn the Warrior over and you'll find the Pleaser. Where the Warrior's response is guarded and abrasive, the Pleaser's is timid and accommodating. Below are some of the forms Pleaser behavior can take:

+ Smiling and saying everything is OK even though you're groaning under the strain of too much work or abusive circumstances

+ Trying to do the impossible (e.g., continuing to try to do everything even when layoffs or attrition force three other jobs into yours)

+ Letting others take advantage of you

+ Feeling superior to the Warriors because you are not engaging in politics the way they are

+ Convincing yourself that you don't really have a choice about how you respond

+ Making sure to be seen in the right meetings

Like the Warrior, the Pleaser wants to hang on to what's in hand. But the Pleaser makes very different calculations. Understanding the difference begins with knowing the Pleaser's mindset:

> *"I will lose out unless I prove my worth to the higher-ups. I cannot make waves. I will be secure if I go along and get along."*

When we engage in Pleaser behavior, we endeavor to ensure our survival by being agreeable. While being accommodating and well liked are not faults in and of themselves, when we employ these tactics habitually, we diminish ourselves and invite others to minimize us, too.

To the extent we pride ourselves on knowing which side our bread is buttered on, we rationalize our feelings about what's going on at work, what we want and need, even how we're being treated. We're the good boys and good girls of corporate life. We are the ones who get on with it, who grin and bear it, who try to be good sports and go along. We may agree with those who think the increased workload is unfair, or that the boss is abusive, but we think those who speak up about it are reckless. We'll keep our mouths shut, thank you.

As Pleasers coping with organizational change, we choose a strategy of fitting in and going along because we convince ourselves it would be difficult if not impossible to replace our job with another one or that a needed confrontation would boomerang. Like the Victim, we fear the loss of income and status, but we Pleasers know to watch our tongue, and "hang in there." We do the things our parents told us would see us through difficult times. But we often find ourselves confused when our strategy leaves us feeling taken advantage of.

Illustration

My work as an executive coach allows me the privilege of getting to know many bright and capable business people. One of the circumstances in which I meet them is pressure-filled. In this setting, several of my coaching colleagues gather with several "high potential" executives to witness those executives in action, then, at intervals, we stop that action to give the executives feedback. It's daunting for the participants, but it can also be transformative for them.

In these intimate exchanges, I see Warriors mostly, but also Pleasers. Here is a story about a person who caught herself in the act of being a Pleaser and leapt into Navigator mode.

One of the interactions requires the executive to take the role of a new boss who has to forge a constructive relationship with an under-performing subordinate. The case material makes clear that the subordinate has been offending coworkers and has, as a result, been losing sales.

Typically, executives approach the situation in a friendly but stern manner; they want to establish their authority but not offend. Trying not to put the subordinate on the spot, they ask a lot of leading questions like "What is your philosophy about the importance of cooperating with your coworkers?" and "Do you think you have fostered enough teamwork?"

After observing that role-play recently, I was giving feedback to an especially perceptive executive who was frustrated that she didn't get anywhere with her direct report.

I asked her, "Suppose you had said to the subordinate something like this: 'Let me back up. I've been asking you a lot of questions. I am now realizing that I should have been telling you what was on my mind instead. Here's what's going on for me: I'm hearing things that make me feel concerned for you. You are making a lot of people angry, people whose support you need to be successful.'"

The executive comprehended my point immediately. She said, "You mean it would be more advantageous for me to have gone deep and been courageous." It took me aback because it was exactly right and so eloquently said. This led to an exceptionally meaningful conversation about the value and power of authenticity. In the midst of that conversation, she said, "You know why I don't take that approach more often? It's because I'm usually too concerned about being a PLEASER." It was her word! She went on to say, "It really takes courage—at least for me—to speak openly and directly."

I briefly shared my view with her about the three choices we have—Victim, Survivor, Navigator. I told her there were two major forms of the Survivor mode: Pleaser and Warrior. I offered the view that, indeed, she took the Pleaser's approach to the interchange. I observed that doing so allows for hiding behind a role, a technique, or a barrage of questions. This is always easier than saying what's really on your mind and using the authority of your own experience.

She smiled broadly and said, "I am moving into a challenging new role. I won't enjoy it and I won't be very effective if I keep trying to please everyone." In our remaining time together, we spoke about how she might accomplish this worthy goal. I came away convinced that she'll do it, too. What a privilege to have worked with her!

Conclusion

The late French biologist, Charles Frederic Dubois, in applying the lessons of a lifetime of studying natural adaptation, summed up the requirements for human growth in a famous statement. He could have been speaking of what *doesn't* happen when we live in Survivor mode. Dubois said, "The important thing is this: to be able, at any moment, to sacrifice what we are for what we could become." Whether we choose the Warrior or Pleaser approach, Survivor mode ultimately limits our growth and development. In Survivor mode, we render ourselves unable even to know we need to let go and take another path, let alone to actually loosen our grip on what we're clinging to and try a new approach. Yet this is precisely what growth requires.

Is letting go a scary thing when the world is changing all around you? It sure can be. It helps to have an alternative, one that doesn't necessarily eliminate fear but which does guarantee a brighter future even though pursuing it requires a bit of courage. We turn now to that response.

Chapter 5

The Navigator Response

> *Life is either a great*
> *adventure—or nothing.*
> *—Helen Keller*

By far the most effective response to workplace change—indeed, to life—is that of the Navigator. Even though only 15–20 percent of us function in this way consistently, everyone is capable of responding to workplace change with the grace and effectiveness of the Navigator.

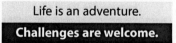

Life is an adventure.
Challenges are welcome.

In this chapter, I will tell you what doing so looks, feels, and sounds like. I will tell you stories about people who functioned in this way and some, including myself, who did not.

Here are three distinctive characteristics of our Navigators:

1. *They have a destination.*

Navigation is meaningless without the idea of an objective; it's the process of getting from one place to the next. Similarly, our metaphorical Navigators set goals and have a bias for action; they're not passive in the face of change.

2. *They have a positive and confident attitude about the future.*

And the good news here is that one's attitude and confidence level can be increased; no one is doomed to negativity and self-doubt.

3. *They use their tools. This has two aspects:*

Using the vernacular of navigation, they take their bearings periodically to see where they are and how things are proceeding and adjust their course based on these data.

In doing so, they realize that subtle feedback (e.g., a feeling, a misgiving) can be just as important as conspicuous feedback (a signpost, a compass bearing).

These are complex, overlapping human abilities, not distinct competencies so let's tease them apart as we explore the complex inner life of the Navigator.

Know Where You are and Have a Destination

When we function as Navigators, we diligently seek to know and accept our current reality, the ups and downs of our lives, what's working and what isn't. We also seek to have clear in our minds a picture of the future we desire. Figure 9 depicts these two tasks.

To the extent that our current circumstances differ from where we're headed, i.e., what we truly desire for ourselves, the tension we

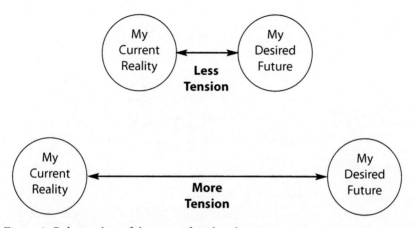

Figure 9 Relationship of distance of goal and tension

feel will mount. In other words, if what we want is significantly different from what we have, we are likely to feel considerable uneasiness. This is also depicted in Figure 9.

We have a choice: we can move away from this tension, or we can put it to use. If we function like a Navigator, we find resources, learn skills, and build dreams that can overcome doubt, fear, and hesitation. Acknowledging what is going on and how we feel about it is the first step. To use a colloquial expression, we "tune in" to our environment and to ourselves when in Navigator mode. We engage in reflection, we are thoughtful. Just as being a navigator in a plane or ship first requires clarity about the starting location before heading to other ports, navigating in life requires creating an interval between our initial perceptions of what is going on and our subsequent responses.

The term Navigator implies that we are committed to arriving at a chosen destination. This might be thought of as our "desired future." As Navigators we choose not only to survive through chaos but also to become a stronger, more capable person because of it, to come out more fulfilled, to create a future of our choosing.

Here is the mindset that enables this:

> *"The situation I am in can be a problematic mess or a challenge-filled opportunity. It is up to me. I don't have complete control over my life and the events that affect me, but if I act like the powerful person I can be, I'll be more likely to make things turn out the way I want them than if I do otherwise."*

It is not easy nor does it come automatically to be Navigator-like. It requires discipline. It is easy is to be Victim-like, and to give up, complain, or blame others. It requires effort to perform an accurate appraisal of our current circumstances and our feelings about them. To make matters more challenging, it's a task we have to keep returning to. Knowing ourselves and making our world work—two interrelated skills—each require tenacity.

The Navigator response is relatively uncommon partly because change tends to evoke uncertainty and with it, fear. As we all know, when fearful the loudest voice within us encourages short-term, myopic solutions. Writer H.L. Mencken once uttered one of my favorite lines when he said, "There is always an easy solution to every human problem—neat, plausible, and wrong." He might have been speaking about the Victim and Survivor modes when he said this, because, during change, what often seems neat and plausible—like hunkering down, trying to out maneuver others, and trying to hold on for dear life—doesn't work very well, at least in the long-term.

When we respond like a Navigator, we resist the temptation to opt for quick fixes. When we're Navigator-like, we know that a creative response is not forthcoming when we let our fears get the upper hand, but being a Navigator entails way more than telling ourselves we shouldn't get upset. In fact, to try to control oneself like this is more Survivor-like than Navigator-like. It's the sort of thing our parents told us when they told us to "settle down," or "get control of yourself." Both are invitations to denial, the tendency to put on blinders.

Maintain a Confident Attitude

How important is a confident attitude, a characteristic central to being a Navigator? I recently encountered a remarkable study that answers the question. It's entitled, "Positive Emotions in Early Life and Longevity: Findings from the Nun Study." It was published in the peer-reviewed *Journal of Personality and Social Psychology*.

The research involved 180 nuns, members of the order of School Sisters of Notre Dame. The nuns, who for their entire adult lives ate nearly the same foods, lived the same lifestyle, had the same reproductive histories, and enjoyed access to the same (good) medical care, nonetheless differed over time along key life dimensions such as mental and physical health and longevity. It is not surprising that women of diverse genetic histories should have subsequently different health and longevity histories. What is surprising is that the longevity of these women could have been predicted 60 years before, merely on the basis of the type of emotional language they used in a short autobiography.

Here's what happened.

In 1932, these nuns received a request to write an autobiography from their Mother Superior who intended to use the stories for educational planning. The nuns were asked to succinctly describe where they were born, what their parents were like, and some significant events in their childhood that led to choosing life in a convent. The completed stories were filed away and discovered by researchers 60 years later. Once discovered, the autobiographies were read and scored for emotional content. Each word and sentence was screened for positive, negative, and neutral emotional meaning using a sophisticated analytical tool.

The results were astounding. The researchers found that for every one percent increase in the number of positive-emotion sentences (e.g., "God started off my life well by bestowing on me a grace of inestimable value..."), there was a 1.4 percent *decrease* in the mortality rate. Further, there was a 2.5-fold difference in longevity between the nuns who wrote sentences containing the greatest number of positive emotional words (e.g., love, relief, gratitude, hope, love, and interest) compared to those who used the least number. Nuns who used the highest number of positive-emotion words lived an average of 10.7 years longer than those who used the least number of such words.

This study is just one of many associating emotionality, outlook, temperament, and longevity. It is compatible with many other longitudinal studies demonstrating that optimism and positive outlook is associated with longer life. Another such study found that how a person explains the meaning of negative events (it's all my fault, it's all others' fault, it's just an event) predicts health effects much later in life.

Studies in this research category have also shown that each fundamental emotional state (some researchers say there are five, some say seven) leads to predictable autonomic nervous system responses, some of which are health-enhancing and some—especially when return to baseline is delayed—are corrosive because they lead to elevated heart rates and blood pressure, increased levels of stress hormones, and so forth. If you have more of feelings such as anger, fear, and hostility, you are far more likely than others who have less of these feelings to experience adverse health effects. Remember the term "Type A behavior"? The central component of Type A behavior is hostility. People who frequently experience hostility are far more likely to develop heart disease than others who don't.

We know from research like the nun study that attitudes and outlooks are hugely important in determining the quality (and length) of our experience. But can a person, especially one who by nature is not necessarily cheery and upbeat most of the time, or one who has just suffered a tragic personal or career loss cultivate the confidence of the Navigator?

Happily, yes. And with an understanding of how to accomplish it comes the good news that experiencing a high level of stress and negative emotionality—at least temporarily—does not mean that you're failing in life or that you can't get into Navigator mode quickly.

Here is what goes on inside the skin of a person functioning in high Navigator mode. I touched on this in Chapter One. When a negative event or even the possibility of a negative event occurs:

- Physiological arousal occurs. If something is negative or potentially negative, it's healthy to respond to it.

- Positive self-talk then begins: "I can manage this," "This is challenging, but there are opportunities here," and "Others have done this, so can I."

- The feelings resulting from the self-talk generate energy and enthusiasm for taking action. You've matched the external event with your own, *self-created* internal event.

- Those feelings mute the potentially adverse effects of the physiological arousal. You've become alarmed, but you've returned to a quieter state, one associated with better health and with more creative thinking.

In Chapter Six I will provide specific guidance on how to develop these functional abilities.

Use Your Tools

Navigators, as I said, use their tools. In explaining this let me tell a story about a time when I didn't practice what I preach. In this experience, I had an opportunity to both be a Navigator (large "N") and a navigator (small "n"). I utterly—and nearly fatally—failed to do either. I'll try to give it a positive ending by passing along some valuable lessons learned.

A friend and I planned a summer hiking trip to the Canadian Rockies. In advance of the trip, we did everything responsible hikers should do: we got ourselves in top physical condition, studied trail guides, identified climbing routes, and carefully selected equipment.

Arriving at the trailhead on our first day, we were full of energy and eager to get going. The many clouds in the sky did not darken our spirits. Our destination, a backcountry lodge accessible only on foot, was nine-miles away, over a steep mountain pass. We would see some of the most spectacular scenery in the world and we couldn't wait to get going.

Exuberant with the freedom that only nature lovers can experience after being cooped up in a big city for several months, we hiked three miles and then paused for a rest at the base of the peak we planned to climb several days later once acclimated to the altitude. In exceptionally high spirits, we made a fateful, impulsive decision: we decided to climb that peak then and there. One of us glanced around at the sky. The clouds were a little thicker now, but it wasn't raining yet and, although the clouds were moving in our direction, they were moving slowly—or so we convinced ourselves.

Racing the weather, we barely beat the clouds to the summit. In one direction, the view was stunning: we could see peak after snow-capped peak for over 30 miles into the distance. But over our shoulders in the other direction and nearly on top of us were the blackest, meanest rain clouds I had ever seen. Far above tree line, we had no cover whatsoever from the lightning that was going to start any moment. If you know anything about mountains and weather, you know that being atop a high peak during a thunderstorm is the last place you should be.

"Let's just get a few pictures and then we'll scoot down," one of us said. CRACK! BOOM! Said the lightning. And boy, did we "scoot": so quickly and in such fear that we lost our way and found ourselves descending by a much more difficult route than the easier one we had taken up. The sea of rocks around us, now saturated with rain, was treacherous.

Then, one of us fell, head over heels down a steep slope, tearing a gash in his knee. There was no time even to cover the wound; we had to descend NOW.

Once at the bottom, relieved and with the worst of the storm passed, we had a dispiriting thought: it is late afternoon, we are still six-miles from the lodge, and we have to hike up and over a steep mountain pass to get there.

There was little conversation as we trudged up that pass. We were physically spent. At the top, we quietly celebrated our easy two-mile descent to the lodge.

Then more troubles. A few hundred yards beyond the top of the pass, the trail forked. At the junction was a signpost that had the name of the lodge on it, but it had fallen over; we had no idea which way to go. Both of us had a map of the area and a compass, but— and here is the crux of this story—we were so exhausted that we did not think to use them! With a 50-50 chance of taking the right path, we chose the wrong one because "it seemed right." Four hours later, drenched with the rain of yet another storm, we stumbled through the dark into the lodge, having added an additional two miles to our trek.

Lessons? Here was a situation in which some of the qualities and commitments of the Navigator were present. For one thing, the intent was vividly clear. The goal was to get to the lodge and have fun doing it. Everything necessary to implement and achieve the goal was at hand: strong bodies, enthusiasm, maps, compasses. Yet the experience was anything but fun. We courted disaster on top of that mountain and made ourselves miserable because we didn't use our tools.

What went wrong? From this example, we can derive some lessons that can be applied to much of life:

- A bias for action, taken to an extreme, can hinder more than help.

- *How* you achieve something is as important as *what* you achieve.

- If you have tools (maps, compasses, feedback from others) that can help you make progress or assess how much progress you've made, *use them*! Be wary of using only your "best guesses." It's important to take your bearings periodically to see where you are and how things are proceeding. Goal achievement is important, but just as important at times is non-action, i.e., reflection. Equally as important as going hell-bent is pausing and reflecting on how well your approach is working; in other words, learning.

From Victim to Navigator

Added together, knowing where you are, using your tools, and maintaining a confident and positive attitude means that you equip yourself to make use of the most amazing organ every to exist: the human brain. Cultivating these abilities will set your cerebral cortex free to separate you from the dinosaurs and from the other humans around you who are responding to workplace change as if they *are* dinosaurs. Rather than belabor what goes into the power of learning, I'd like to tell you another story to illustrate it. It's a story that illustrates how anyone can use adverse events at work to grow. It's the story of someone I admire who used the experience of painful organizational change to become a deliberate learner.

His name is Mark, a former client. His story shows that learning, while powerful and life-changing, can also be painful and take us on a path that's anything but straightforward.

It began with reorganization at his company, when Mark was offered a job that he considered beneath his abilities. He felt insulted because the job he was offered was one he had held four years before. The message given by his employer through this offer was that Mark had a set of needed skills, but his skills were less valuable due to Mark's interpersonal problems.

This "demotion," as Mark called it, came with a bit of relief—at least he wasn't getting fired—but it enraged him. For one thing, he would now be reporting to people he had hired, a circumstance he considered demeaning. For another, his opportunity to work with clients he had cultivated in remote parts of the company would now be curtailed.

Told of the decision, Mark stormed out of his boss's office and didn't come back the rest of the day. He sulked at home, so much so it worried his wife. Returning to work, he was "polite" and "civil" for several weeks but no more than that.

Ironically, it enraged Mark to hear his boss say that Mark's anger made him hard to work with. Mark didn't appreciate the irony, though; he just considered his boss unfair and ungrateful. As happens so frequently, this was a case of career disruption stemming not from a problem with technical competencies, but from interpersonal *incompetencies*. But Mark had a different interpretation. In his view, he was the victim of politics and jealousy.

Mark's seething anger gradually gave way to depression as he made the shift to his new, less demanding assignment. His wife tried to get him to talk about his distress, but to no avail. Coworkers steered clear of him.

Finally, after some weeks of difficulty sleeping, Mark mentioned the problem to his family physician during a routine check-up. His doctor recommended sleeping pills. This alarmed Mark and he said so. "Those things can be habit-forming, can't they," he asked the doctor. "Well," the doctor said, "Your other option is to see a psychiatrist. You seem to need one or the other. You aren't sleeping because you're upset about something. There's nothing wrong with you physically. I will tell you, however, that you're courting an ulcer. You need to relax."

Mark left without a prescription or the name of a psychiatrist to call. The idea that he "needed" to see a psychiatrist or take pills challenged his sense of control over his life. He always saw himself as able to make the best of situations. He thought of himself as a competitor. But he was failing this time, at least in his estimation.

For a few days after the doctor visit, Mark felt even more depressed and continued to lose sleep. Rousing himself to some kind of problem-solving action was almost impossible.

Mark did manage, over several weeks, to update his résumé. Asking a trusted coworker to look at it, he told his friend with characteristic anger about the "stupid" doctor who told him he needed to see a "shrink." "There's no way I'm going to stay at a company where I'm not appreciated," Mark said. "This job is making me sick."

His friend responded by saying, "I don't think you need a psychiatrist, either, Mark. I think you need to be more honest with yourself." His friend stayed calm and looked him in the eye. "Look, Mark, you've been told that you're hard to work with and it's cost you something career-wise. Surely it's not the first time you've ever heard this. Perhaps this time you can find a way of learning something from it." His friend implored him to use this painful situation as an opportunity to learn.

The conversation ended when Mark made a derogatory remark about how his friend seemed to be turning against him, too. But Mark was finally at a point where he couldn't deny the feedback from his boss, the doctor, and his friend.

That night, Mark began to open up to his wife about his pain. As he began to tell her about the events at work, he said, "I don't think I've ever been this low before. And the worst part is I'm confused. Do you think I have an anger problem?" She told him the truth.

For the next few weeks, Mark found that the courage to face the painful realities of his current situation grew as he battled his reluctance to face his feelings: he was angry, yes, but on reflection, he realized that his anger was often a mask for insecurity and fear. Through anger he could put others on the defensive and buy time so he could come to a decision about his own path forward. He wouldn't have to think on his feet, something that was always difficult for him. And he realized that while he hated his boss and his circumstances, if there were a better path forward, he would have to identify it; no one else would or could.

Mark told me that he began to feel a gradually growing sense of inner peace as he allowed the possibility that perhaps he *was* difficult to work with. He put his résumé writing on hold for a while, setting the goal of learning about himself. He made an appointment with his boss specifically to discuss his working style. "I don't have to agree with him," he told himself. "But maybe I can learn something."

Ultimately, Mark became very clear about what made him a troublesome employee. Opening more to his wife, he learned that his competitiveness, anger, and perfectionism were not confined to work; they were also problems at home. For a while, he felt discouraged because he didn't think he would be able to change himself or that, if he did, anyone at work would notice or appreciate the effort. He sometimes felt washed up.

At his boss's suggestion, Mark went to a seminar on interpersonal communication that he had refused to attend months before. The seminar provided a simple framework for understanding how his style pushed people away. He could also see how it hurt him at home and the course helped him begin to identify other means of influencing people.

Mark found that when he put forth effort to cooperate with others those initiatives were appreciated and made getting things accomplished easier. For the next year, Mark volunteered for projects in his department to deliberately to demonstrate his newfound commitment to teamwork. He was open with his teammates about his aim to be more cooperative. It paid off. He was offered a new, more rewarding role when his division opened a new business line.

Optimism or Pessimism?

Mark moved from pessimism to optimism as he became more Navigator-like. At first, he was convinced that there was no way he could comfortably continue working in his company. He wanted to take flight. He was convinced that he could not change his behavior, or if he did, that others would fail to recognize his efforts to do so. His behavior as a Victim was typical in that he expected everything to work out poorly.

To expect everything to work out poorly is irrational. But let's turn the coin over. When we respond to circumstances like a Navigator, do we expect everything to work out well, which is just as irrational? No. As the popular saying goes, "Stuff happens." None of us are in complete control of how things turn out.

Even so, when we're Navigators, we do find ways to look on the bright side of things. A key distinction separating the Victim and Navigator mindset is the interpretation of events: is it an insurmountable problem or is it a challenging but potentially golden opportunity? From the one vantage point, we are hamstrung; from the other, we concede the difficulty and choose to deal with it anyway, and in the process affirm our abilities and ourselves.

The connection of these observations to the Navigator response has to do with a simple yet profound psychological fact: *those who believe they will make the best of a difficult circumstance are those most likely to do so.* When responding like Victims, we perceive the control over our circumstances to be external to ourselves, when responding like Navigators, we perceive it to be internal; *we* determine how well or poorly we fare.

As Navigators, we perceive the world as one of *potential* scarcity and *potential* abundance, understanding that whichever comes to pass depends, in great measure, on our own initiative and outlook. As Victims and Survivors we have the expectation that we'll either get nothing or we'll have to make disappointing tradeoffs.

In the story of Mark, above, we get a glimpse into how the Navigator sounds, that is, the kind of things a Navigator says. Below is a list of other statements I've heard employees in Navigator mode make:

> "*This change is based on business realities. The change is not intended to make me miserable.*"

> "*My function was considered unimportant until I proved how much revenue it could generate.*"

> "*I'm not going to wait until my boss asks me to plan the next step in writing this newsletter. I'm going to identify the options and think them through and present him with some ideas for exploration.*"

> "*Nobody can tell me I should feel great about this because I don't, but I am determined to make this the best thing that ever happened to me.*"

Conclusion

As a metaphor, the concept of land, sea, or air navigation applies perfectly to what is required to work our way through life. We need to know where we're headed, but we need to know where we're starting from, too. We also need some kind of route or itinerary to guide us. Finally, we need to use our tools—our brains, our inner knowing—to fine tune and course-correct at every step.

Do you want to feel more confident to handle what life offers you and to create the future you want? Then get better at learning. Learning permits us to sidestep needless pain and fruitless striving as our worlds evolve. If we are competent at learning, we are intentional seekers of the resources, skills, ideas, philosophies, and connections required for fulfillment. You will learn a simple but powerful means to turbo-charge your learning in the next chapter.

Chapter 6

Strategies for Navigating Organizational Change

If you don't develop a strategy of your own, you become a part of someone else's strategy.
—*Alvin Toffler*

Workplace change is a challenge to everyone, but let's face it: if you are in a position to guide organizational change, to decide that it's necessary and on what timetable it should take place, you will struggle less with it than those who are expected to carry out that change. This is so because it's taking place on your schedule and you're in charge. Still, organizational change calls on both the decision-makers and the implementers to cope with the discontinuity that follows, even though the demands of change may be different for both groups. For one thing, each group has to let go of the old ways of doing things, and then has to deal with the discomfort as transition bumps along.

The question to consider is this: how do you stay health—physically, mentally, and even spiritually—while continuing to be productive during organizational change? In other words, how do you get and keep yourself functioning in the Navigator zone? Figure 10 answers this question. My intention in this chapter is to provide you with very practical suggestions that will enable you to accomplish each of the three tasks noted in the figure.

First, notice the words at the top of the figure, "Stand up to change" and at the bottom, the words "Make the best of change." I'm sure you'll agree that there is a world of difference between the two ideas. "Stand up to change" implies surviving it, while "Making the best of change," suggests leveraging it for some higher purpose. As I've said before, there is nothing wrong with the Survivor mode as a *temporary* measure; indeed, it's vastly better than dealing with change from the Victim mode. Choosing Survivor mode for a time can enable us to find some balance during uncertain times.

To make the best of change, we have to go beyond merely coping with it, however. Like it not, we are expected by our employers to continue to be productive during change. In this chapter, I will provide several suggestions to meet the demands of this phase as well.

Finally, making the best of change means that we go well beyond merely coping with change to actually using the change as an opportunity to create a future of our choosing. In terms of ultimate rewards, this is where the "pay dirt" is. This is Navigator mode, full out.

Stay Alive and Well

Herb Shepard, a founder of the field of organization development, once wrote an article entitled, "Rules of Thumb for Change Agents." Rule #1 was, "Stay Alive." Herb wrote, "This rule counsels against self-sacrifice on behalf of a cause that you do not wish to be your last." Herb was addressing those leading change, but the rule is

STAND UP TO CHANGE

Stay alive and well

Maintain positive eating, sleeping, and exercise habits.

Try to be grateful—for everything.

Take a balanced view of the past—and the present.

Consider seeking professional help when you've gone for two or three weeks without let up in emotional distress.

Master the demands of the moment

Be patient with yourself and others: change takes longer than it takes.

Negotiate work demands.

Build and use supportive relationships.

Learn, learn, learn.

Create the future you want

Try to be a part of the solution, not part of the problem.

Talk to yourself—positively.

Develop and practice an approach to creating your future.

MAKE THE BEST OF CHANGE

Figure 10 A progression of change management tactics

even more important for anyone who is attempting to cope with the changes that others are driving.

I am using the term "Staying alive and well" mostly metaphorically, but it bears pointing out that the stress of change, especially the stress of change created by others, can threaten our physical health, especially if we are prone to intense experiences of anxiety, impatience, worry, or anger. The strategies in this section will help you buy time to comprehend what is really changing and what isn't, and to minimize the intensity of these feelings.

Take Care of Your Physical Self

A well-fed and well-exercised body best withstands the stress of change. For one thing, healthy muscle fiber is the most metabolically active tissue in the body and will help you process the stress hormones that inevitably accompany workplace change. Staying fit will help you cope.

Even if you typically maintain a healthy diet and exercise regularly, if you're like most people, you will be tempted to let those good habits lapse when change is occurring at work. When change is underway, it is often accompanied by the need to put in longer hours, causing further disruption to our exercise and eating habits. This is the very time when these habits are most essential.

I don't intend to tell you how to eat or exercise, but I will tell you this: according to most health counselors, getting 20-30 minutes of exercise three-four times each week is an absolute minimum when your workplace is completely stable, let alone when it's in flux. According to the American College of Sports Medicine, less than two-thirds of adults in the U.S. get their recommended minimum amount of exercise per week: 20-30 minutes of moderate intensity exercise at least two to three days/week, but ideally five days/week. What if you're not an exerciser and your idea of a good meal is a few glazed doughnuts? Push away from those calories and start walking.

Get a Good Night's Sleep

According to the most recent poll by the National Sleep Foundation, Americans get an average of about 6.7 hours of sleep during a weekday whereas most health professionals think eight is the right number for most people. More alarming (pun intended), the number of people who sleep less than six hours per day has increased by 60 per cent in the last ten years while those getting more than eight hours per day has dropped significantly. In explaining these phenomena, experts point to the stress caused by the 24-7 work world and economic woes. These findings align with a survey by the American Psychological Association that found that 52 percent of Americans are losing sleep at night from stress.

Consider Meditating

Many people hear the word "meditation" and think it's a religious practice employed by men with long, grey beards on mountaintops, sitting in awkward positions. In fact, meditation is the act of focusing your mind on a simple thought, sound, or image for a few minutes. You don't even have to be sitting as meditation can be done while walking. Meditation can take many forms and can be profoundly beneficial as a means of alleviating stress.

The physiological benefits of meditation were conclusively demonstrated by Dr. Herbert Benson of Harvard's Medical School in the 1970s. Dr. Benson wanted to know if a simple, nonreligious practice of meditation could help those diagnosed with diabetes reduce their need for insulin. He taught the subjects to sit with their eyes closed for 20 minutes while saying the word "One" to themselves. They were told to expect their minds to wander off—and to resume saying the word if it did—until the time had elapsed. Before and after the meditation period, subjects' blood sugar levels were monitored. The subjects quickly learned the technique and required less insulin as a result. (This was not a permanent change: if they stopped meditating, their blood sugar again rose in most cases.)

The purpose of meditating is twofold: it's a way to alleviate the effects of daily stress and tension, and it's a way to focus the mind.

Pertaining to the latter, you can use meditation simply as a relaxation technique, but you can also use it for deep introspection into your life, a process for which I will introduce later in this chapter ("The Daily Trek"). By meditating, we induce what Herbert Benson called "the relaxation response," a physiologically beneficial state characterized by lowered blood pressure, the decrease of stress hormones, changes in brain wave patterns, and cardiological rest. By spending time in this state, your body stops producing stress hormones and efficiently metabolizes the stress hormones already present in the bloodstream.

Many books have been written about meditation and its benefits. Even though it was published a long time ago, I would recommend Herbert Benson's *The Relaxation Response*. Your local library almost certainly has a copy or two.

Be Grateful—for Everything

In describing the Navigator, I used to use the slogan, "Life is difficult, misery is optional." I liked the formulation because it emphasized a teaching point I wanted to make about how life is taxing and that it's helpful to accept the fact. I subsequently decided that, "Life is an adventure. Challenges are welcome" was more in tune with the spirit of the Navigator because it was more upbeat and confident. Still, it's useful to consider the idea that misery truly is an option.

One of the best ways I know of to stay misery-free is by cultivating an "attitude of gratitude." Try to be grateful—for everything, even your grief, your impatience, and your anger.

Let's explore this a little.

From a strictly cultural perspective, one of the primary contributions of religion is to help people deal with adversity. It turns out that most religions see a connection between gratitude and stress reduction. Consequently, most religious groups have many songs of gratitude. My favorite is from the Unitarian tradition and is called, "*For All That Is Our Life.*"

The first verse of this song starts out in a rather conventional way: "For all that is our life we sing our thanks and praise; for all life is a gift..." So far, not much to argue with.

It's the third verse that both confronts and shows the true wisdom of songwriters Bruce Findlow and Patrick L. Riley. How's this for a stanza in a song of gratitude: "For sorrow we must bear, for failures, pain and loss...we come with praise and thanks..."

How could sorrow, failures, pain, and loss be appropriate objects of gratitude? Are the songwriters masochistic? The answer is in that first verse: all life is a gift. When in the proper frame of mind, all of life can be valuable: life's disappointments, grief, even despair.

When I was a young man, I had it in my head that at some point, I would have "arrived" at a place of ultimate satisfaction in my life. I would be esteemed by my colleagues, certainly wealthy or at least affluent, socially confident, and, well, invincible. In this fantasy, all my insecurities and fears would have vanished.

Instead, I find as I grow older that the insecurities are still there— although I can now better control both the circumstances that provoke them and the intensity of my reactions to them—and I feel more vulnerable to pain and loss. I have seen my parents die, a dear brother die, and I have even seen some of my dreams die. Adding to the vulnerability, each day I grow more attached to my wife and children, and therefore, more exposed to the potential loss of the gifts they give me.

But at the same time, life is immeasurably richer because I have many loving relationships and also because I have had relationships with loved ones and then lost them. I have grieved and I have valued that grief. And because I was unable to fulfill some of my most cherished dreams, I had other life experiences that have taught me a great deal and provided their own gifts.

Would I choose a life without pain if I could? Would you? Frankly, I'd consider it—and then would choose a life of adventure and try to be grateful for the twists and turns that come along—for all of them.

Take a Balanced View of the Past—and the Present

I woke up with a poem on my lips this morning, one I'd literally written in my dreams, at least most of it. It's about the importance of valuing the past but the greater importance of moving on from it. The first three lines (the best ones, I think) are all I can remember of the dream version of the poem. I wrote the other lines after waking.

> Your past is passed.
>
> No pill can its remedy be,
>
> no drink its fixer.
>
> Draw deep its bitterness,
>
> expel its allure.
>
> Blare the trumpets.
>
> Bury it.

My poem may not rival Robert Frost, but it nails the idea for me: we owe it to ourselves to derive value from the lessons of the past, but also to remember that the virtues of the past probably weren't as good as we recall them.

There have been times in my life when living in the past seemed more fulfilling than living in the present. These have been times when I was carrying a load of chronic, low-level anxiety. For instance, yesterday. I heard the words "anxiety," "scared," and "fear" probably 10 times while listening to radio accounts of the current jobless numbers. This no doubt made its contribution.

When the workplace changes in ways that feel threatening, it's hard to remember that the past was not all rosy and that the present is not all bad. But keeping perspective is crucial.

I have had the opportunity to work with hundreds of people whose jobs were ending. In the early stages of an impending layoff, the tendency of workers to idealize the past is almost irresistible. Overnight, aspects of work that once were the source of frequent complaints are forgotten and a keen nostalgia grows for the rest of it.

Working with employees in this situation, I have asked them to make drawings depicting what their company was like when they first became a part of it—the THEN drawings—and drawings showing what the company is like now—the NOW drawings. Invariably, the THEN drawings of the "old timers," the employees with the greatest years of service, show smiling faces, sunny skies, and stick figures hugging one another. Their NOW drawings show storm clouds, frowns, and even knives in people's backs. It's a very useful exercise because after some in-depth discussion, everyone gets the point: the past wasn't that good, the present isn't that bad.

In one of those seminars, a participant made the following statement. I'm not sure where he heard it and I've never heard it since. It captures the tendency to want to glorify the past.

Now is the Past that Someone in the Future Longs to Return to.

I love that statement! In just a few words, it sums up what it's like to be human in the midst of change, especially the change that others create and that we have to deal with.

It's important during change to be careful not to idealize the past and to strive to identify what's good about the new situation, too. Having said that, it's also important to mourn the passing of the old situation, especially if it's been truly meaningful for us. In fact, doing so can enable people to let the past go more easily and move on in their transition. One client really helped his organization do this in advance of closing down a plant. He scheduled a whole day of celebration for the past accomplishments of the plant and at the end of the day, there was a tearful, touching, and healing "funeral ceremony" for the plant.

Here are a few more lines about the past, this time in the context of the future, eloquently stated by a great philosopher, George Santayana:

> We must welcome the future
> knowing that soon it will
> be the past.
> And we must respect the past
> knowing that it was once
> all that was humanly possible.

Consider Seeking Professional Help when You've Gone for Two or Three Weeks Without Relief from Emotional Distress.

Organizational change is challenging, even stressful. But challenges and even stress aren't necessarily bad things. On the other hand, depression, prolonged, intense anger, chronic agitation and tension, inability to think, and other psychological and physical symptoms are problems—especially if they persist over time.

Everyone has periods of feeling blue or upset or angry. If you have a brief episode once or twice a month, this is pretty normal. But if you have gone for two weeks or more without let up in emotional distress, it's probably time to seek the advice of a mental health professional.

You may remember from Chapter One that more than half of Americans say they are frequently troubled these days by feelings of irritability, fatigue, insomnia, and depression due to work and workplace issues. You may also recall that while this is true, nearly half of Americans say they would be uncomfortable asking someone they know for help in managing stress and almost six in 10 would be very reluctant to reach out for professional advice to manage the problems stress is creating in their lives. It's Navigator-like to reach out for help when you're distressed. As I said in the last chapter, use your tools!

How might you know if you should seek counseling from a professional? The American Psychological Association offers the following guidelines:

- You feel an overwhelming and prolonged sense of sadness and helplessness, and lack hope.

- Your emotional difficulties make it hard for you to function from day to day. For example, you are unable to concentrate on assignments and your job performance suffers as a result.

- Your actions are harmful to yourself or to others (or you are *considering* doing harm to yourself or others). For instance, you drink too much alcohol and become overly aggressive (or are *considering* becoming aggressive).

Most health plans include a mental health component. If you're feeling stressed by workplace change (or anything else), use this benefit. If you are covered by health insurance but aren't sure how to access the benefit, ask your Human Resources support person or call the insurance carrier. As we've been learning in this book, talking to a supportive person can do wonders for your outlook. Reaching out to a mental health professional does not mean you're weak or unable to cope; it may mean you're doing something smart. If you have no health insurance coverage, reach out to community mental health resources and inquire about pastoral care at your church or synagogue. Use your tools! Don't suffer in silence.

Again, stay alive

We would be remiss not to mention that during change you might find yourself in its driver's seat. Perhaps you are a manager or a change champion associated with a transition effort and you believe wholeheartedly in its merits. Here's more from Herb Shepard, a great master of organizational change:

> *The counsel [to stay alive] is not to say that one should never take a stand, or a survival risk. But such risks should be taken as part of a purposeful strategy of change, and appropriately timed and targeted. When they are taken under such circumstances, one is very much alive…Staying alive means staying in touch with your purpose. It means using your skills, your emotions, your labels and positions, rather than being used by them.*

In other words, be passionate and go for excellence, but choose your battles and be prepared not to let the quest for improvement consume you.

Master The Demands Of The Moment

Change tests everyone. One perspective is that this is nature's way of asking, "Who's willing to put up with the struggles and discomfort in order to get the goodies?" You want to be one of those people.

> *Be patient with yourself and others: change takes longer than it takes.*

William Bridges writes books about organizational change, about how to get from the old to the new. His name perfectly aligns with his work! Bridges made two enormously helpful contributions to our understanding of the subject.

First, he pointed out that there is a huge difference between *change*—when something old stops and something new starts—and *transition*—the human, psychological process of coping with change. As Bridges put it, "It isn't the changes that do you in, it's the transitions." The former, says Bridges, are situational, the latter, psychological. Second, Bridges observed that the psychological process of transition unfolds in essentially three phases.

The first of Bridges' three phases of transition, ENDING, is often filled with strong feelings of loss and reactivity to those losses, especially if the change is not necessarily of your own choosing. During this phase, we tend to long for and idealize the past as we explored in the section above. We can feel sad and even angry as we attempt to grasp the meaning of events.

Mercifully, while intense, the time we spend in ENDING is rather short compared to the next phase which Bridges calls the NEUTRAL ZONE. In this phase of transition, we haven't fully let go of the old ways yet nor have we fully embraced the new. It is an awkward time of refitting expectations, behaviors, habits, and methods. The old hasn't quite died, the new isn't fully operational. We're in the wilderness. It pays to remember that Moses led his flock for 40 years through the desert before they got to the Promised Land!

Most of us long for Bridges' third phase of transition: the NEW BEGINNING. This is when we emerge from the wilderness with fresh energy and fresh commitment for the new ways.

My point in reviewing Bridges' work is simply this: change—excuse me, *transition*—unfolds in predictable ways and it is easier to be patient with the time it takes if we understand the process. And once we do understand the process, we can help others and ourselves as they work their way through the phases of transition. Below are a few practical guidelines. If you're at all intrigued with these ideas or you are in a position of authority and are driving change that others have to deal with, do yourself a favor and read Bridges' book, *Managing Transitions*.

ENDING

* Expect resistance to change. Try to appreciate the loss and grief that resistance represents.

* Respect the past; don't toss it out in favor of the new even if you think the new is far better.

* Be clear about what's changing and what isn't.

* Try to see how letting go makes room for and enables the new.

NEUTRAL ZONE

* Normalize the awkwardness of the Neutral Zone; understand it and respect it. Try to be patient with your lowered productivity if this occurs.

* Establish short-term improvement markers and goals so that you can experience the reality of making progress through the Neutral Zone.

* Reach out for social support and, if you're a manager, pull people together for group sessions that allow people to describe how they're feeling. (Do this in the Ending Zone, too.)

* Use the chaos of the Neutral Zone to learn new skills and try new approaches.

NEW BEGINNING

* Manage your energy: just because you've emerged from the awkward Neutral Zone doesn't mean you have limitless get-up-and-go. Burnout can be caused by enthusiasm, too.

* Create symbols that typify the new vision.

* Celebrate having arrived in the "Promised Land."

Negotiate Work Demands

Researchers have long known that there are three basic forms of work stress: ambiguity (you don't know what's expected of you or you don't know what is going to happen), conflict (mostly the interpersonal variety), and overload (too much to do, not enough time to do it). Guess which is the most likely when organizational change is at its peak? Overload. But the other two are usually present during change, too.

Of the three, overload is the easiest to deal with but many people do almost nothing either to prevent or to manage it constructively.

My counsel here is pretty simple: if you're feeling overloaded, whether because a coworker has been laid off and you're now doing two jobs, or for any other reason, push back, but do so respectfully and thoughtfully.

Most employers don't want employees, especially their best employees, to resent their work. Thus, most managers will be receptive to a conversation about work demands. If you are feeling that you can't possibly do everything that's expected of you, say so. Again, do so in a way that invites problem solving, not in a complaining way.

For instance, instead of saying, "Hey! What do you think I am, a perpetual motion machine?" say, "I understand the importance of what you're asking me to do. Help me set priorities on the other work that's already on my plate."

If you're overloaded or are about to be, it's likely that your manager will want to know that you have doubts about your ability to complete all the work he or she is expecting of you. And if there is a real chance that you won't be able to deliver, don't remain silent and hope your boss is forgiving. Let your boss in on the dilemma and communicate your need for help in sorting through the priorities.

Build and Use Supportive Relationships

When they experience trauma, most people want to talk about it. Whether it's an illness, a car accident, the death of a loved one, or a disruptive change at work, people need to express themselves. It's the most natural psychological process imaginable and it has healing power. In short, people need the comfort of others. Psychologists call it "social support." To show you the prevalence and power of social support in people's lives, I went to an online psychology site and typed in that phrase in the search box. Below are the first four article titles (of over a thousand!) that came up:

- Parents Of Children With Rare Diseases Benefit From Intensive **Support** Programs

- Social **Support** Negatively Linked To Prognostic Marker For Ovarian Cancer

- Psychological **Support** Helps Adolescents with Chronic Fatigue Syndrome

- Social **Support** Improves Mental Health After a Traumatic Health Care Intervention

Think about it: when big change is afoot at work, what happens? Productivity tends to drop. Why? Because people are talking about the change instead of working. The counsel in this section is to take care of yourself by talking to others—in a particular way: by first stating your pain and then by stating one small step you are going to take to address that pain.

Let me explain. People have the most to say during the phase of transition that Bridges calls ENDING because this is when we feel an acute sense of loss. If our inner Victim is going to emerge, this is the most likely time. As I've said many times in this book, we need to be tolerant of our inner Victim, but we also need to put limits on it. While social support is important and useful, congregating with others for the purpose of complaining is not. So my first bit of advice is to avoid people who just want to complain and when *you* complain, do so wisely!

In other words, allow yourself to complain if you feel the need, but try to avoid endless, negative whining. Set yourself up for success with your friend by first saying something like, "I am so frustrated I could scream. Do you mind if I just complain for two minutes? I'd like to rant for just a bit and then I'd like your help in thinking through how I can find something valuable in this or at least make a constructive response." Almost invariably, what follows will be helpful in some way.

Suppose the situation is reversed and someone who isn't in Navigator mode comes to you and begins complaining bitterly and at length about something at work. What can you do to protect yourself? Try this: say to the other person, "You seem (upset, angry, frustrated, enraged, irritated). How would you like me to respond? Would you just like me to listen for a couple of minutes, or do you want my advice?" In so many words, it tells the other person that a) you only have a couple of minutes for listening to their complaints, and b) they have a choice of two constructive responses: simple empathy or advice-giving. What if their energy is so intense they just want to go on and on? Say something like, "You know Bob, I don't really know how to help you except to ask this question: what are you going to do to take good care of yourself?" This implies that they aren't doing so by complaining and you're close to finished listening.

Learn, Learn, Learn

I have spoken extensively in this book about my view that learning is the most powerful thing a person can do so I won't belabor the point here. It might be useful, however, to identify the specific opportunities for learning that are available to someone in Navigator mode during organizational change. I will clarify those opportunities by Bridges' phases of transition:

ENDING

+ Pay attention to the feelings you are having and the choices you make about how to deal with them. Try to identify role models, i.e., people you work with who cope creatively with transition and change. Consider adopting their methods.

+ Learn as much as you can about the strategic and business reasoning behind the organizational changes taking place. Sometimes, knowing the rationale behind change can enable you to feel more tolerant of its disruptive effect and to position yourself as an ally of management in the change process, perhaps advancing your own career in the process.

NEUTRAL ZONE

+ Carve out time for yourself to step back and reflect on what you're learning about change, transition, new systems and processes, and your own skills.

+ If courses and seminars are offered to help workers learn new systems, get the most from them. You will never waste time learning new skills; the very process of learning generates energy and ensures vitality.

- When you encounter disappointments and setbacks, strive to see them as the beginning of a new period of opportunity and growth not as insurmountable failures.

- If your boss isn't doing so, urge him or her to gather your team to review progress and share learnings as well as best practices in dealing with the changes taking place. Share your own experiences with coworkers whether your boss convenes the group or not.

NEW BEGINNINGS

- Learn new ways of helping people visualize a positive and productive future.

- Learn how to work cooperatively with others to create that future.

Create the Future *You* Want

Getting and staying in the Navigator mindset requires being in touch with all aspects of life: the joys as well as the pain and suffering that life inevitably entails. It is especially important to get in touch with the pain and suffering we cause ourselves. We can't eliminate *all* pain, but at least we can minimize or eliminate that kind.

Let's admit to one thing: it's far easier and more rewarding to reflect on what's working in our lives, on what makes us feel good and whole and uplifted, than to take our pain seriously, to find meaning in it, and to learn from it. Doing these things requires inner resources of a particular kind. I think of these as spiritual resources. If this term makes you uncomfortable, hang in there with me for a moment. I am not trying to convert you to any religious belief or get you to believe in a higher power: unless we're talking about your *own* higher power.

When in Victim mode, we run from pain or fight with those whom we believe are the cause of it. When in Survivor mode, we try to ignore pain or attempt to beat it into submission through our will. When in Navigator mode, we move toward the pain, seeking to understand and learn from it. Doing so requires a kind of fortification that is available only from the higher, inner human powers.

Another way of saying all this is that when everything is changing around you and you are at risk of losing your center, the best thing you can do is create some change of your own, even if that merely means you change your mindset from that of a Victim or Survivor to that of a Navigator. If you're overwhelmed with the effort required to keep up with the new initiatives coming from the outside, launch some of your own initiatives even if this is simply taking care of yourself in a better way than you have in the past.

Allow me to reveal a little secret, however: this is easier said than done, unless prior to stressful change you have devoted time to learning the skills that the Navigator response entails. Here is the good news: these skills are relatively easy to learn if you spend regular time with them. Below, I will tell you how to cultivate them.

In this section, I am going to address each of the activities that being in Navigator mode requires of us if we're to create the future we want. Those activities are:

Try to be a part of the solution, not part of the problem

Talk to yourself—positively

Develop and practice an approach to creating your future

These activities can be addressed collectively by describing a daily practice that can help you stay grounded, continue learning, and create the future at work (or off-the-job) that you really want. I call it The Daily Trek, a journey that you take in your mind once or, ideally, twice, each day.

The Daily Trek

Some people want life to be easy and to enjoy the benefits of the Navigator mode with little or no effort. I don't have much to offer them.

I met such a person recently while giving a talk on the ideas in this book. He asked me a great question: "What is the single most important thing a person can do to become and remain a Navigator?"

I didn't hesitate for a nanosecond. My answer was, "Take daily time in contemplation, gratitude, and affirmation." After explaining what I meant and noting that it requires a willingness to be still and to listen—on a daily basis—my questioner replied, "I'm an action person, not a reflective person. What should I do?"

Again, I did not hesitate: "Become more reflective."

I went on to ask him to consider how lame his stance would be if he had just heard a lecture on the benefits for longevity of exercise or the benefits for dental health of daily flossing. I asked him, "Would you tell a physiologist or a dental hygienist that they need to give you different advice because you don't like exercise or taking care of your teeth?" He got the point.

Functioning in Navigator mode is not automatic. It can become habitual, but like any good habit, you have to cultivate it. If you wait until all hell breaks loose to learn how to remain calm in the midst of trouble, you're likely to find it very hard to achieve your goal. I have a friend who is fond of saying, "You have to dig the well before you're thirsty." This is exactly what he's talking about. But here's the good news: you can do this work without leaving your house.

The Daily Trek is a mental exercise in which you take a kind of excursion in your mind at least once each day. If your life is especially stressful, twice per day is more beneficial. If you go to my website, as indicated in the box below, you can download a podcast that will guide you through the process. You can play it on any mp3 player (iPod or equivalent) or burn it to a CD.

Let me walk you through it then I'll review each segment in greater depth.

Before doing this exercise the first time, it is a good idea to have a few goals in mind, things you want to achieve both on- and off-the-job. I suggest that you spend some time creating this list thoughtfully and writing your goals in a particular way: in the form of what has been called an "affirmation." An affirmation is a statement about what you want to create, worded as if it's already true. Here are a few affirmations that relate to making the best of organizational change. Use them as is or modify them to fit your specific needs:

- I am taking good care of my physical health during this change.

- I am taking a balanced view during change: the past was not all rosy; the present is not all bad.

- I am keeping my options open.

- I am searching for several responses to the changing circumstances, not just one.

- I am avoiding either-or thinking.

- I am staying open to my feelings during change and realizing that while they might be painful, my feelings are potentially useful sources of information for me.

- I am using all painful experiences as opportunities to learn.

- I am spending as much time as I can with people who support and sustain me. I am avoiding the complainers.

- I am initiating some positive change of my own as the most constructive response I can make to the changes initiated by others.

• In this period of transition, I am taking time to mourn the passing of the old situation as I strive to embrace the merits of the new.

Again, if you are undergoing highly stressful change, my advice is to engage in the Daily Trek exercise twice each day: once before you start your day, once right before you go to sleep. Find a quiet time and place where you won't be interrupted. Yes, you can do this in bed, but be aware that you don't get the benefits if you fall asleep! Having a timer handy can be very useful, but if it has a loud ring, put it under a pillow so it doesn't jar you when time is up. Set it for 20 minutes.

1. Relax deeply

Get yourself as relaxed as you can. Relaxation has two benefits: it enables you to dissipate tension, and it permits you to focus your mind. There are any number of ways to induce a state of relaxation but the simplest method is to simply focus intently for a few minutes on your breath: count ten breaths, then count ten more, then count ten more, etc. Repeat this for at least five minutes.

2. Honestly, and with compassionate acceptance, review your answer to the question, "What's it like to be me right now?"

For two minutes or so, allow yourself to know how you've been feeling. Consider what's occurred in the time interval since you last did the exercise. How did you feel during those activities? Don't be judgmental of what comes up. Instead, be compassionate and accepting. Allow yourself to experience the emotions that go along with your answer to the question. Use the language of emotions. Instead of saying, "I have no goals right now," say to yourself, "I feel aimless and sad."

As many people have trouble identifying their feelings, here is a list that might be useful to you. Psychologist Paul Ekman, author of many lauded books on human emotions, has identified seven emotional states as most basic to human experience. They are listed below along with some synonyms:

Fear—Terror, dread, horror

Sadness—Grief, sorrow, unhappiness

Anger—Aggravation, rage, fury

Joy—Delight, happiness, contentment, bliss

Surprise—Shock, astonishment, upset

Disgust—Repulsion, hatred, abhorrence

Contempt—Disdain, disapproval, scorn

3. Review everything in your life that you feel grateful for

People who are appreciative of the positive things in their lives enjoy more social support, have fewer accidents, heal faster when sick, and achieve more in their lives. In this segment, review everything in your life that is working, that makes you smile, that nourishes you, and that warms your heart. Perhaps your heart is aching because you just got laid off. You review the pain of this in step #3, but in this step, you acknowledge your gratitude for those who have extended an offer of support to you during this time. Even if most of your life feels likes it's falling apart, find something—anything—that you feel grateful for and dwell on it for a few moments.

4. State some affirmations about the future you desire

The study of high-achievers in various fields shows a common habit: successful people, whether in business, sports, or in their personal relationships, have intensely clear and positive images of their goals. Thus, when you observe a successful entrepreneur, a remarkable athlete, or an admirable parent, you are observing a person who knows what he or she wants and has a vivid picture of it in their mind, one they invest with energy.

If things aren't working in your life, whether on- or off-the-job, you have a choice: you can focus on the distress these things are causing or you can focus on what you want instead. Do what mentally healthy people do: dwell on the positive things you want. Using the affirmations you created earlier, articulate your heart's desire, focusing on it as if it's already come to pass. As you do so, you increase the likelihood that it will become reality.

After you say each affirmation, picture your future as if this has already come true. If, for example, your affirmation has to do with maintaining your physical health, picture yourself working out or taking a walk. If your affirmation has to do with exchanging your resentment for openness and peace, picture yourself going through your day in a tranquil manner.

By the way, after you've gone through this exercise a few times, you will have committed your affirmations to heart. In the meantime, it's perfectly OK to open your eyes and read them off an index card or piece of paper.

5. *Say to yourself, "All this, or something better, is now becoming the reality of my life."*

This is what I like to think of as the "granddaddy of all affirmations." Once you've stated each affirmation and visualized each one as if already true, say the affirmation above to yourself. After this, simply spend the remaining few minutes enjoying the state of rest, peacefulness, and vitality you've created in yourself.

Conclusion

I sat down to write the conclusion of this book and wasn't sure what to say. Looking for inspiration, I glanced to the bookshelf and saw a volume there that I recommend to anyone who is introspective and loves beautiful books. It's called, *WHO ARE YOU: 101 Ways to See Yourself*, by Malcolm Godwin. The author helps you answer the title question every two pages, using a different framework or lens for each "look" at yourself. Without taking a stand as to which perspective is better than the others, he takes you on a tour of yourself using vehicles as diverse as Sun Signs, somatotypes, Enneagrams, and 98 other concepts. On every other page is an "assessment" designed to help you identify which type you are. The illustrations are first-rate.

The book you've just read, of course, raises this question, too: who are you? I've introduced you to the metaphor of the Victim, Survivor, and Navigator, and I've made the claim that existing inside each of us are each of those actors. Even more important than "who are you" is the question, "Which *one* are you most of the time?" Each of us is a deep and complex web. We are unique. We have many aspects. And we can choose which aspect of ourselves leads our inner team.

Get *The Daily Trek* podcast

Download a free podcast from my website that guides you through the entire Daily Trek. It takes just over 15 minutes to listen to the whole podcast. During that time, I will guide you through a simple relaxation exercise and help you focus on a few of your goals and, because you did this exercise, you will be more likely to achieve them.

To download *The Daily Trek,* go to:

RichardMcKnight.com.

Chapter 7

Worksheets and Exercises

This chapter contains a number of worksheets, surveys, and models that can help you think through what it's like to be you right now at work and, if that is not 100 percent to your liking, to potentially enable you to identify pathways that will lead to a more fulfilling and even thrilling life.

A Survey of Opinions

© 2009, Richard McKnight, Ph.D.

Below are groups of three statements. Place a check mark in the blank before the one statement in each group that *most* represents your views. There are no right answers. Don't worry about trying to be consistent. To get a total, you must check one statement in each group.

	1.	Change brings good fortune about as often as it creates bad outcomes.
	2.	Change usually provides people with an opportunity for growth.
	3.	Change usually turns out poorly for most people like me.
	4.	Luck plays almost no part in a person's success or failure.
	5.	Having good fortune determines the outcome as often as not.
	6.	Without luck you won't get anywhere.
	7.	In a conflict, it's usually best either to take a firm stand or to move away.
	8.	In a conflict, it's usually best to try to hear the other person's point of view and then express your own.
	9.	In a conflict, it's best to try to minimize the differences between yourself and others.
	10.	Having feelings like sadness or anger is unavoidable.
	11.	Having feelings like sadness or anger means you've lost control.
	12.	Having feelings like sadness or anger means other people or events have made you feel that way.

13. Politicians can be made to be responsive and responsible to the voters.

14. Politicians are untrustworthy no matter what voters do.

15. No matter what, there will always be some good politicians and some corrupt politicians.

16. If you admit mistakes, others will probably take advantage of you.

17. Admitting to your mistakes is a good way to start learning.

18. It never pays to call attention to our errors.

19. The best things in life are often unreachable despite how hard you try.

20. The best things in life are pretty much there for the taking as long as you put forth effort.

21. The best things in life are sometimes attainable, sometimes not.

22. Life is a thrilling adventure.

23. Life is one problem after another.

24. Life is a series of good days and bad days in about equal measure.

25. Most people are trustworthy.

26. Most people are pretty honest, but it still pays to be watchful.

27. Most people will take advantage of others if they can.

	28. People can affect but not control the quality of their lives.
	29. People have no real control over their lives.
	30. People control the quality of their lives.
	31. No matter what life turns up I am sure I can deal with it.
	32. I can deal with most difficulties.
	33. I am frequently overwhelmed with life's challenges.
	34. Most people will help you if you need it.
	35. Most people let you down.
	36. Many people are dependable, many are not.
	37. When negative things happen, worse things will probably follow.
	38. When negative things happen, some sacrifice will be necessary.
	39. When negative things happen, better things are probably right around the corner.

Scoring

In the grid on the following page, circle the numbers of the statements you checked above, then put the total number of checks in each column at the bottom.

Victim	Survivor	Navigator
3	1	2
6	5	4
7	9	8
12	11	10
14	15	13
16	18	17
19	21	20
23	24	22
27	26	25
29	28	30
33	32	31
35	36	34
37	38	39
Total	Total	Total

The total in each column indicates the extent to which your outlook parallels that of the Victim, Survivor, and Navigator mindset. Please be clear: this is not a diagnostic "test"! It is not intended to slap a label on you or anyone else. No one is purely a Victim, only a Survivor, or exclusively a Navigator. The most important thing is to use your scores to deepen your understanding about the Victim, Survivor, and Navigator ways of thinking.

The survey assesses attitudes about the following:

+ How to get ahead (luck, hard work, etc.)

+ How to resolve conflict

+ Authority figures

+ Getting along with others

+ Quality of life

+ Likelihood of success in life

+ Trustworthiness of others

+ Change

+ Causation (luck)

+ Likelihood of problems creating good/bad future

There is no right way to analyze your results as long as it leads to deepened understanding of who you are. If you scored below 8-9 in the Navigator category, study your results very closely. Where did you choose Victim or Survivor perspectives? Challenge yourself to examine your attitudes in those areas to see how you're undermining yourself. Share your results with a friend. Explain the three mindsets and ask for their views about how you operate: "Do I function more as a Victim, a Survivor, or a Navigator?"

I would enjoy hearing your reaction to this little survey. If you have suggestions for improving it, I'd love to hear them.

Interpretation and Commentary

S	1.	Change brings good fortune about as often as it creates bad outcomes.
N	2.	Change usually provides people with an opportunity for growth.
V	3.	Change usually turns out poorly for people like me.

A person operating in the Victim mode expects the worst. The person in Survivor mode is more hopeful. Still, both bet on the present. The Survivor, fearing that the future will disappoint as often as not, is at least open-minded. Navigator mode calls on us to see the possibilities in change for opening doors that otherwise would be closed. Of course, Navigators know that the kind of change that matters most comes from within. But even then, there are no guarantees. Anwar el-Sadat, third President of Egypt, knew this. Sadat, who along with Menachem Begin signed the Camp David Accords, said, "He who cannot change the very fabric of his thought will never be able to change reality." Many extremist Egyptians despised Sadat's call for peace with Israel. They ultimately killed him. Life is challenging, even the life of a Navigator.

N	4.	Luck plays almost no part in a person's success or failure.
S	5.	Having good fortune determines the outcome as often as not.
V	6.	Without luck you won't get anywhere.

Research on goal attainment shows that the highest achievers place no faith in luck at all; they see themselves as the sole cause of their success. Ever notice those long lines for lottery tickets and how it's the same people every week? Society's highest achievers don't stand in lines like that. They know that randomness (luck) plays a part in everything, but since they can't influence it, they don't wager—except on their own abilities. Robertson Davies, Canada's great man of letters, once wisely said to a graduating class, "What we call luck is the inner man externalized. We make things happen to us."

V	7.	In a conflict, it's usually best either to take a firm stand or to move away.
N	8.	In a conflict, it's usually best to try to hear the other person's point of view and then express your own.
S	9.	In a conflict, it's best to try to minimize the differences between yourself and others.

Item 7 offers fight/flight as the only two alternatives, while item 9 urges caution and conciliation, the stance of the Survivor, Pleaser variety. The Navigator's choice is to listen politely and then to express his or hers own views. Steven Covey, in his famous Seven Habits of Highly Successful People, said it this way: "Seek first to understand and then to be understood."

N	10. Having feelings like sadness or anger is unavoidable.
S	11. Having feelings like sadness or anger means you've lost control.
V	12. Having feelings like sadness or anger means other people or events have made you feel that way.

Feelings are rich sources of information—at least potentially. Some people, Navigators, use their feelings to inform their decision-making. The way a friend puts it, "If I'm feeling really angry, I want to be the first to know, not the person I'm about to yell at." When in Victim mode, we can be in touch with our feelings but we tend to act them out, not to learn from them. In Survivor mode, we tend to rationalize them or deny them.

N	13. Politicians can be made to be responsive and responsible to the voters.
V	14. Politicians are untrustworthy no matter what voters do.
S	15. No matter what, there will always be some good politicians and some corrupt politicians.

This set gets at our sense of inner power and vulnerability with respect to authority figures, in this case politicians. Victim mode is the place of cynicism: everyone is suspect. Survivor mode has us believe there are two categories of authorities: the good ones and the bad ones. Whether true or not from an objective point of view, those who live in Navigator mode are optimistic about most things, even their ability, when acting in concert with others, to bring the political class to heel. Steven Biko, South African anti-apartheid activist who died in police custody said, "The most potent weapon of the oppressor is the mind of the oppressed." His meaning, stated in the lexicon of this book, was if you can induce a Victim or Survivor mindset in the populace, you've gained control over the people. (By the way, in the past few decades, Americans' distrust of politicians has about doubled according to most surveys.)

V	16. If you admit to mistakes, others will probably take advantage of you.
N	17. Admitting to your mistakes is a good way to start learning.
S	18. It never pays to call attention to your errors.

No one sets out to make errors or mistakes but we all do. What happens then? The Victim tries to hide it or cover it up. Why? A person in Victim mode will tell you others aren't forgiving, but the real reason is fear of looking bad, losing face, getting in trouble, etc. Survivors hide out, too, and if some failing comes to light, self-protection sets in. I love this quote by Colin Powell. It summarizes the way of the Navigator: "There are no secrets to success. It is the result of preparation, hard work, learning from failure."

V	19. The best things in life are often unreachable despite how hard you try.
N	20. The best things in life are pretty much there for the taking as long as you put forth effort.
S	21. The best things in life are sometimes attainable, sometimes not.

The goodies are sometimes attainable, sometimes not, says the Survivor within. This is better than the counsel of the inner Victim who would have us not even try to get the good stuff in life. On the other hand, our inner Navigator knows that if there are "breaks" in life, we make them, bringing a decided bias for action to life along with optimism. The famous hockey player, Reggie Leach, sums up the Navigator's view: "Success is not the result of spontaneous combustion. You must set yourself on fire."

N	22. Life is a thrilling adventure.
V	23. Life is one problem after another.
S	24. Life is a series of good days and bad days in about equal measure.

Here's another quote from sports, this time from Tug McGraw, the relief pitcher who threw the winning strike in the 1980 World Series for the Philadelphia Phillies. McGraw knew—based on his team's loss of the Series in 1973—that, "Some days you tame the tiger. Some days the tiger has you for lunch." But the idea of life's being a thrilling adventure was Helen Keller's. Her exact words were, "Life is either a daring adventure or nothing."

N	25. Most people are trustworthy.
S	26. Most people are pretty honest, but it still pays to be watchful.
V	27. Most people will take advantage of others if they can.

Some people go through life in a perpetually guarded state because they look around them and see people ready to let them down, hassle them, cheat them, disappoint them. If I mistrust myself, I am much more likely to mistrust others. Not to say that there aren't nasty people out there but Navigators find that what goes around tends to come around: if you lead with trust, you tend to get trust back. Ronald Reagan, when dealing with Soviet Chairman Mikhail Gorbachev, loved to quote the Russian proverb, "Trust, but verify." Personally, my favorite saying on the subject is by American painter and naturalist, Walter Anderson: "We're never so vulnerable than when we trust someone—but paradoxically, if we cannot trust, neither can we find love or joy."

S	28. People can affect but not control the quality of their lives.
V	29. People have no real control over their lives
N	30. People control the quality of their lives.

This is a tricky one; read it closely. One the one hand, Helen Keller said that security—a form of control—was a "superstition," noting that it simply doesn't exist. But if the pursuit of security is fruitless, how about control? Isn't this the same thing? It gets back to one's perception about who is the source of greatest control in one's life and what they have control over. Given that complete control over anything is mythical, where is the preponderance of control in your life: within you or outside of you? This book has been putting forth the view that while you may not have total control over outside events in your life, you do have control—at least potentially—over its internal events.

N	31. No matter what life turns up I am sure I can deal with it.
S	32. I can deal with most difficulties.
V	33. I am frequently overwhelmed with life's challenges.

Mother Teresa, a world-famous Navigator, had a knack for summing up much of life in a sentence. When asked about her faith, she said it was complete because, "I know God will not give me anything I can't handle." Then she added, "I just wish that He didn't trust me so much." What more can I say?

N	34. Most people will help you if you need it.
V	35. Most people let you down.
S	36. Many people are dependable, many are not.

This set addresses the trustworthiness of others. On that subject, Frank Crane, actor, screenwriter, and director observed that, "You may be deceived if you trust too much, but you will live in torment if you don't trust enough." Cadets at West Point are taught about trusting, too, via this Navigator's maxim: "Risk more than others think is safe. Care more than others think is wise. Dream more than others think is practical. Expect more than others think is possible."

V	37. When negative things happen, worse things will probably follow.
S	38. When negative things happen, some sacrifice will be necessary.
N	39. When negative things happen, better things are probably right around the corner.

Why isn't abundance as likely as more bad stuff when negative things happen—at least emotional abundance? Statistically, if something terrible happens, it is extremely unlikely that more terrible stuff will follow despite the Victim's fear that bad things come in three's. Here is Walter Anderson again: "Bad things do happen; how I respond to them defines my character and the quality of my life. I can choose to sit in perpetual sadness, immobilized by the gravity of my loss, or I can choose to rise from the pain and treasure the most precious gift I have—life itself."

Job Stress Index

Following is a list of 27 changes that often occur in a workplace transition. Using the scale below, place a number in each blank to show the degree to which you've been troubled by that of change in your organization. (If you have not experienced a particular change, put a zero.)

0 = Not occurring or doesn't bother me at all
1 = Bothers me very little
2 = Bothers me a moderate amount
3 = Really bothers me; stressful
4 = Extremely bothersome; exceptionally stressful

	1. Working longer hours
	2. Greater work load
	3. Being surrounded by "nay-sayers" and complainers
	4. Having doubts about the future prospects of the organization
	5. Having doubts about the future prospects of your own job
	6. Increased responsibility
	7. Increased responsibility with decreased authority
	8. Uncertainty about what is expected of you
	9. Being held more accountable for the way things turn out
	10. Demotion to a lesser position
	11. Being unable to get information you need to do your job effectively
	12. Your job has changed such that you no longer do the most interesting aspects of your assignment

	13. Having to report to someone who has less experience or seniority than you have
	14. Having to make decisions that will adversely affect the lives of people you care about
	15. Being assigned new duties that are "over your head"
	16. Feeling conflict between your job and your family life
	17. Being unclear about the scope and responsibilities of your job
	18. Being sure that the amount of work you have to do may interfere with how well it gets done
	19. Increased job complexity
	20. Decrease in the amount of control you have over how your job gets done
	21. Greater time pressure
	22. Feeling unable or unwilling to "fit" into the changed company culture
	23. Unclear reporting relationship
	24. Difficulty getting approvals
	25. Change in work location
	26. Loss of company identity or name
	27. Change in or loss of company benefits
	TOTAL

Now, find your score on the scale below to get a picture of how stressful your job circumstances are these days:

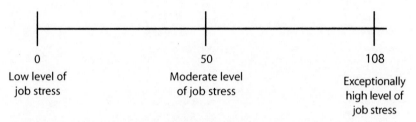

0
Low level of
job stress

50
Moderate level
of job stress

108
Exceptionally
high level of
job stress

If your score is between 81-108 (you put either a three or four for each answer), it is likely that you are carrying a heavy load of job stress right now. You probably feel pain—physical and psychological—associated with the changes unfolding in your workplace. Obviously, if your score is less, you've been less troubled and your immediate circumstances may not be that bad.

Stress Symptoms

Having some stress is essential to good health and contentment yet too much stress can be harmful and result in various types of symptoms. Circle any of the symptoms below that you are prone to experiencing when under stress, whether or not you are suffering from them lately. *Then, go back and put a star by those you are suffering from these days.*

One way of making sense out of this is to remember that we all respond to stress in distinctive ways. For example, while your coworker might have indigestion when under stress, you might never have this problem; but you may have back pain. Partly, this is determined by heredity, partly by personal habit. By paying attention to how your body reacts to tension, you have the advantage of early warning signs: you can alter your responses and head off potentially debilitating stress breakdowns. Try to think of these signs and symptoms as sources of useful information: they are!

Spiritual	Mental
• loss of purpose • cynicism • sarcasm • apathy • being unforgiving • mood swings • martyrdom	• moodiness • feeling vulnerable • negative self-talk • boredom • inability to think • lack of creativity • obsessive thoughts • forgetfulness • scattered concentration • apathy • memory problems
Physical	**Emotional**
• chest pain • abdominal pain • stomachaches • digestive upsets • appetite change • fatigue • sleep disturbances • increased use of over-the-counter drugs • pounding heart • heart palpitations • rapid heartbeat • weight gain/loss • frequent colds • colitis (irritable bowel) • skin rashes • allergies • headaches • constipation • twitches/tics/jitters • accident proneness • teeth grinding • dizziness	• panic • depression • anxiety • dread • bitterness • bad temper • worrying • lack of intimacy • nightmares • cry easily • self-contempt

Optimal Stress

Stress itself is not a bad thing. In fact, we need some stress in our lives to function: to breathe, to stand up straight, to get out of bed in the morning. As stress increases, so does productivity—up to a point. However, going beyond an optimal level of stress can result in a decrease in productivity.

Make an X on the graphic below to show where you are right now with respect to the stress you feel in your life. Are you in the "Drone Zone" where you feel under-stimulated and bored at work? Or are you over-stressed and in the "Burn Out Zone"?

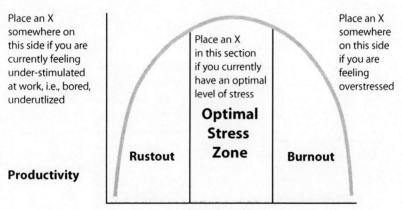

Place an X somewhere on this side if you are currently feeling under-stimulated at work, i.e., bored, underutlized

Place an X in this section if you currently have an optimal level of stress

Optimal Stress Zone

Rustout

Burnout

Place an X somewhere on this side if you are feeling overstressed

Productivity

Amount of Stress

105

Dealing with Conflict:

A Catalog of Navigator-like and Less-Than-Navigator-like Workplace Behaviors

I am Less Navigator-like When I...	I am More Navigator-like When I
• Try to please others and have them think I agree with them. • Say one thing and mean another. • Complain about having too much to do. • Shift my priorities based on who is in the room or who is screaming the loudest. • Try to look busy so my manager does not give me more work. • Speak ill of others without confronting the person who could do something about the issue. • Venting negative/bitter frustrations without taking action to solve the problem. • Come out "sideways" about resentments, wrapping messages in sarcastic humor. • Use flight/silence as a main way to handle uncomfortable issues. • Close off dialog on specific topics. • Employ manipulation or bullying tactics.	• Am authentic—honest with others and myself. • Get clear on top priorities for work and how this work fits into the company goals. • Ask questions to clarify the weekly and monthly priorities. • Renegotiate work demands if overwhelmed. • A few days in advance of the deadline: "I've looked at my schedule over the next few days. I would like you to help me establish the priorities so I complete what is most important for the department. I'm willing to work extra hours this week if needed to get the work done, and I need your guidance." • Talk directly with decision makers who can influence an issue without engaging in sideways conversations with people who are not able to help. • Think through issues and create opportunities to discuss issues with the other party without shutting down.

Index

CPSIA information can be obtained at www.ICGtesting.com
Printed in the USA
BVOW02s0722150216

436745BV00001B/4/P